I0813619

Praise for *Using Technology in a Differentiated Classroom*

Using Technology in a Differentiated Classroom is crafted with the practitioner at the forefront. Teachers are elevated to the role of designer and given the right questions to ask to better reach each student through multiple avenues, including content, process, and products. Kilbane and Milman have a deep understanding of educational technology and the power it holds for differentiated instruction.

—**Emily Dillard, EdD**
Director of Instructional Technology,
Alexandria City Public Schools, Virginia

Kilbane and Milman's *Using Technology in a Differentiated Classroom* should be on every teacher's bookshelf as an invaluable how-to resource for leveraging technology in their teaching. This book explains current understandings of technology's potential to address diverse learner needs, providing a step-by-step and practical approach to effective teaching design. Educators will find it an essential guide for creating engaging, inclusive, and personalized learning experiences in today's digitally equipped classrooms.

—**Teresa S. Foulger, EdD**
Professor of Educational Technology, Arizona State University

Although differentiated instruction has always been accepted as "best practice," practitioners often struggle to implement it with fidelity. Utilizing a logical, well-designed framework, Drs. Kilbane and Milman provide teachers and other education leaders with a design orientation that demystifies differentiation while providing countless methods to weave it into their planning. The post-pandemic timing of this important work is particularly prescient given learners' increasingly varied needs and the countless technological tools now available to assist our teachers in supporting all learners.

—**Mark Secaur, EdD**
Superintendent, Smithtown Central School District
and President, New York State ASCD

Differentiation is an educational game-changer, but it can be challenging to take from theory to practice, especially where edtech is involved, so it was a delight to read a book that explains how to do this in such an accessible way! Whether you're a newbie at using technology or a tech pro, this book provides a comprehensive look at how to differentiate lessons with technology along with insightful examples, tips, and applicable strategies. A recommended read for any educator!

—**Martha A. Ramirez**, author of *In-Class Flip: A Student-Centered Approach to Differentiated Learning*

Drs. Clare Kilbane and Natalie Milman build on Carol Ann Tomilson's seminal work on differentiated instruction by encouraging teachers to think of themselves as design professionals and highlighting the value of combining differentiation, design, and technology. They demonstrate how digital technologies can support every aspect of designing for differentiated instruction. The clear language, concrete examples, and many visuals make this book a must-read for educators striving to take an innovative, design-oriented approach to differentiation in the classroom.

—**Kara Dawson, PhD**
Professor of Educational Technology and Associate Director for Graduate Studies, University of Florida

This book validated my own beliefs and experiences in differentiation and provided me with enriching new technology tools and best practices to use with all types of learners.

—**Meggie Scogna,** Student Support Coordinator, Alexandria City Public Schools, Virginia

This book is a must-read for all educators from preK to higher education! Rather than focusing on technology first and the student second, *Using Technology in a Differentiated Classroom* shows how to design learning experiences that put the student front and center. It also explains how technology can help create a more inclusive, student-centered, and inviting classroom community. This book should be the go-to resource for anyone interested in learning how to differentiate teaching and learning. It offers a toolkit of ideas, tips, resources, and tools that educators can immediately apply to their practice. I give it my highest recommendation!

—**Torrey Trust, PhD**
Professor of Learning Technology, Teacher Education, and Curriculum Studies, College of Education, University of Massachusetts Amherst

Using Technology in a Differentiated Classroom

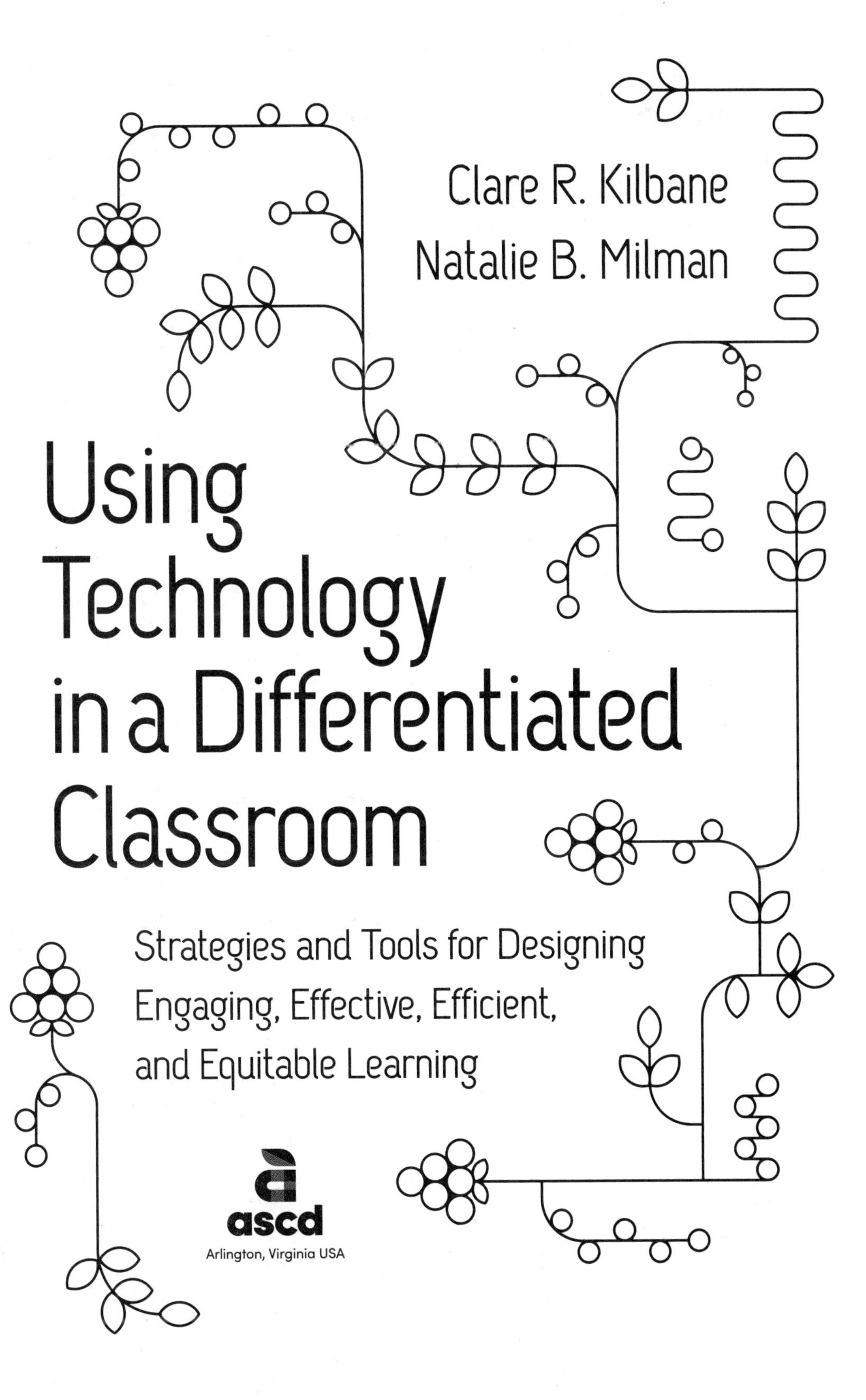

Clare R. Kilbane
Natalie B. Milman

Using Technology in a Differentiated Classroom

Strategies and Tools for Designing Engaging, Effective, Efficient, and Equitable Learning

ascd
Arlington, Virginia USA

2800 Shirlington Road, Suite 1001 • Arlington, VA 22206 USA
Phone: 800-933-2723 or 703-578-9600
Website: www.ascd.org • Email: member@ascd.org
Author guidelines: www.ascd.org/write

Richard Culatta, *Chief Executive Officer;* Anthony Rebora, *Chief Content Officer;* Genny Ostertag, *Managing Director, Book Acquisitions & Editing;* Mary Beth Nielsen, *Director, Book Editing;* Katie Martin, *Senior Editor;* Georgia Park, *Senior Graphic Designer;* Valerie Younkin, *Senior Production Designer;* Shajuan Martin, *E-Publishing Specialist;* Christopher Logan, *Senior Production Specialist;* Kathryn Oliver, *Creative Project Manager*

Copyright © 2025 ASCD. All rights reserved. It is illegal to reproduce copies of this work in print or electronic format (including reproductions displayed on a secure intranet or stored in a retrieval system or other electronic storage device from which copies can be made or displayed) without the prior written permission of the publisher. By purchasing only authorized electronic or print editions and not participating in or encouraging piracy of copyrighted materials, you support the rights of authors and publishers. Readers who wish to reproduce or republish excerpts of this work in print or electronic format may do so for a small fee by contacting the Copyright Clearance Center (CCC), 222 Rosewood Dr., Danvers, MA 01923, USA (phone: 978-750-8400; fax: 978-646-8600; web: www.copyright.com). To inquire about site licensing options or any other reuse, contact ASCD Permissions at www.ascd.org/permissions or permissions@ascd.org. For a list of vendors authorized to license ASCD ebooks to institutions, see www.ascd.org/epubs. Send translation inquiries to translations@ascd.org.

ASCD® is a registered trademark of Association for Supervision and Curriculum Development. All other trademarks contained in this book are the property of, and reserved by, their respective owners, and are used for editorial and informational purposes only. No such use should be construed to imply sponsorship or endorsement of the book by the respective owners.

All web links in this book are correct as of the publication date below but may have become inactive or otherwise modified since that time. If you notice a deactivated or changed link, please email books@ascd.org with the words "Link Update" in the subject line. In your message, please specify the web link, the book title, and the page number on which the link appears.

PAPERBACK ISBN: 978-1-4166-3321-1 ASCD product #120002 n10/24

PDF EBOOK ISBN: 978-1-4166-3322-8; see Books in Print for other formats.

Quantity discounts are available: email programteam@ascd.org or call 800-933-2723, ext. 5773, or 703-575-5773. For desk copies, go to www.ascd.org/deskcopy.

Library of Congress Cataloging-in-Publication Data
Names: Kilbane, Clare R., author. | Milman, Natalie B., author.
Title: Using technology in a differentiated classroom : strategies and tools for designing engaging, effective, efficient & equitable learning/Clare R. Kilbane, Natalie B. Milman.
Description: Arlington, VA : ASCD, 2025. | Includes bibliographical references and index.
Identifiers: LCCN 2024029054 (print) | LCCN 2024029055 (ebook) | ISBN 9781416633211 (paperback) | ISBN 9781416633228 (adobe pdf) | ISBN 9781416633235 (epub)
Subjects: LCSH: Individualized instruction. | Computer-assisted instruction. | Educational technology.
Classification: LCC LB1031 .K4127 2025 (print) | LCC LB1031 (ebook) | DDC 371.33/4—dc23/eng/20240730
LC record available at https://lccn.loc.gov/2024029054
LC ebook record available at https://lccn.loc.gov/2024029055

34 33 32 31 30 29 28 27 26 25 1 2 3 4 5 6 7 8 9 10 11 12

To our teachers,
especially Carol Ann Tomlinson,
and to the teachers and students
who learned through—and from—
the COVID-19 pandemic.

Using Technology in a Differentiated Classroom

1

Approaching Differentiation as an Educational Designer

This chapter covers…

- What differentiated instruction is and how it affects contemporary teaching and learning.
- Why a design orientation supports more effective differentiation.
- How to capitalize on the technology you use when designing for differentiation.

The term *transformative* may be overused, but what better word is there to describe certain events? Experiences such as falling in love, becoming a parent, and traveling in a different country affect a person's life and sense of purpose in profound ways. Although a transformation's dramatic nature becomes apparent only at a specific, climactic moment, most transformations are long in the making. All at once everything changes… but only *after* the covert convergence of many imperceptible forces over time.

For educators, the experiences of 2020—particularly the pivot to remote instruction—were truly transformative. Developments that had been building for decades were accelerated and augmented and will now continue to influence educational practice for years to come. Anyone involved in education during the COVID-19 pandemic has emerged from it with new understandings, sophisticated skills, and powerful competencies. There is no returning to a pre-pandemic profession, with its limited instructional options and one-size-fits all approaches to supporting students' success.

We now have the opportunity to apply what we have learned to teach with greater creativity, impact, and efficacy. And now more than ever, educators can benefit from expanding their capacity to achieve the goals of differentiated instruction by integrating practices from the field of instructional design (Kilbane & Milman, 2014). This effort will allow teachers to deploy technology in more powerful ways to support the success of every learner.

For more than 20 years, differentiated instruction has empowered educators to adjust various elements of practice in response to the needs of academically diverse students in their classrooms. It has offered new and experienced teachers alike a flexible framework to guide adaptation of the content, process, products, and environments associated with classroom instruction (Tomlinson, 2014). Given the pandemic's effect on educational practice, new awareness of equitable instruction's role in promoting social justice, and the expanding number and variety of technologies available for teaching, differentiation has even more relevance for teachers today.

The key to more effective differentiation is adopting a "design orientation"—an approach that applies strategic, systematic thinking to the challenge of designing instruction to address diverse learners' needs. Teachers who work in this way, acting as what we refer to as "educational designers," implement differentiated instruction that makes learning more equitable, efficient, effective, and engaging. Functioning as an educational designer also enables more powerful integration of technology for the purpose of supporting learners and their learning.

What Is Differentiated Instruction?

Differentiated instruction (DI) is an approach to education that places students' needs at the center of instructional decision making. Rather than prioritizing curriculum coverage, teacher preferences, or other goals, in a differentiated education setting, the priority is each student's optimal growth. Effective differentiation relies on an educator's ability to plan instructional experiences that respond to the natural differences that exist in each person, especially those involving individual interests, motivators, and preparedness for learning. Teachers who differentiate instruction well plan proactively to address these variations, routinely engaging in specific practices that allow them to accurately anticipate—and, therefore, more fully accommodate—their students' differences. They also analyze students' various assets and incorporate them into instructional plans in a way that enriches and extends learning. The intentional use of formal and informal inquiry (e.g., assessments, observation, questioning, other forms of investigation) is a hallmark of differentiated learning environments. Educators who differentiate effectively are experts in both their academic content areas and the students they serve (Tomlinson & Imbeau, 2023).

Teachers who are effective differentiators also share the belief that each child has potential and can succeed with the right support. With this as their inspiration, these teachers cultivate a broad repertoire of instructional strategies and practices that allow them to flexibly address the specific and changing needs of their students. Over their career span, skilled differentiators expand, deepen, and refine their practice, becoming more proficient and potent practitioners. They benefit from connecting with a network of like-minded professionals and collaborating with colleagues in their school and beyond to share ideas, materials, challenges, and achievements.

Tomlinson's Framework

Carol Ann Tomlinson's first book on differentiation, published in 1995 and now in its third edition as *How to Differentiate Instruction in Academically Diverse Classrooms* (2017a), is widely considered the seminal work on differentiated instruction. In it, she explores the meaning of differentiated instruction and operationalizes a process teachers can use to address academic diversity. In that book, and in her other publications, Tomlinson delves into the philosophy, principles, and practice of differentiation and presents a conceptual model that encourages educators to think about instruction in ways that emphasize their role as instructional decision makers. Recognizing the control educators have over the essential elements associated with instruction (i.e., content, process, product, and affect/environment), she explains how these might be adjusted in response to an educator's understanding of three dimensions of student variance: interest, readiness, and learning profile (i.e., students' preferred approaches to learning). Teachers build an understanding of their students that is necessary to support sound decisions through a combination of informal and formal information gathering characterized by interactions, observations, and various types of assessment.

Tomlinson (2017b) also identifies five key elements of differentiation:

- An invitational learning environment;
- A high-quality, focused, and meaningful curriculum;
- Assessment used in a way that informs teaching and learning;
- Instruction that is responsive to student variance in readiness, interest, and learning profile; and
- Classroom leadership and management that allow for both predictable routines and flexibility.

By sharing concrete examples of these principles in practice, Tomlinson's work illuminates the process of differentiation and thus empowers educators to implement differentiation in their own classrooms, adopting their instruction to build on students' unique differences. Teachers who employ Tomlinson's differentiated instruction model with fidelity can create instructional experiences that honor students as individuals and equip them to succeed both in school and in life beyond it. In this way, teachers who differentiate well provide equitable instruction and opportunity.

A community of practice has developed around Tomlinson's framework and vocabulary—her way of articulating the philosophy, principles, and practices that characterize differentiated instruction (see Figure 1.1). By working together and gradually becoming more connected via conferences, the internet, and professional networks, educators have, in effect, created a professional knowledge base and expanded and refined the practice of differentiation.

When developing learning experiences, teachers who follow Tomlinson's framework consider ways to adjust four aspects of classroom instruction. Essentially, these are the targets of differentiation:

1. **Affect and the learning environment.** This includes the physical learning space—physical or virtual classrooms, learning management systems, outdoor spaces, virtual breakout rooms—and also

how the space functions and feels (e.g., learning community culture) and how everyone in it engages with one another.

2. **Content.** This is the "input," the material students need to learn. It also encompasses how the students access the information or content they are learning (e.g., via print books, online resources, problem sets).
3. **Process.** This is how students learn and what they do as they *appropriate* the content (make it their own). It may involve the activities students perform while making sense of, retaining, and applying the content learned, whether working in cooperative learning groups, using tools (e.g., calculators), or rotating through learning centers or breakout rooms.
4. **Product.** This is what students create or do to demonstrate what they have learned. It involves a culminating output (e.g., skits, multimedia reports, presentations) that allows students to rehearse, extend, apply, and express what they have learned in a unit of study.

FIGURE 1.1
Dimensions of Differentiated Instruction

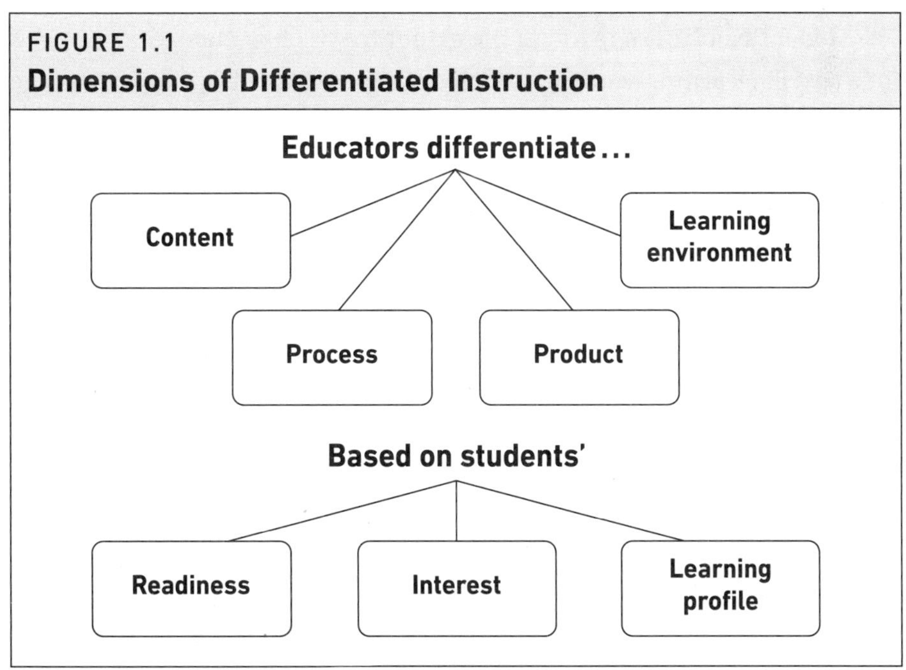

Source: Adapted from *How to Differentiate Instruction in Academically Diverse Classrooms* (3rd ed.), by C. A. Tomlinson, 2017, p. 20. Copyright © 2017 ASCD.

Incorporating Student Variances

Teachers who differentiate instruction with fidelity to Tomlinson's framework rely on what they know about their students as they make decisions that will contribute to achieving the goals they have for these students. The success of each student is an important priority, and most other decisions follow from it. For example, when deciding how much time to allot for a particular unit, a teacher's plans for pacing might consider the differing amounts of prior knowledge the students possess and the preparation they need to be ready for successful learning. For this reason, teachers plan to incorporate assessment at all stages of the learning process and intentionally develop relationships with students in order to stay tuned in to their students' evolving strengths, needs, and interests.

When adjusting the four aspects of classroom instruction (learning environment, content, process, and products), Tomlinson (2017a) advises considering three dimensions of student variance: readiness, interest, and learning profile (see Figure 1.1). Although students differ in many ways, these dimensions are the ones most relevant to motivating and accommodating students' unique talents and their learning needs.

Student **readiness** involves the extent to which a student is prepared for a specific learning sequence. It encompasses students' prior knowledge and existing skills as well as their dispositions. For example, students' readiness for learning about telling time consists of their understanding of the concept of time and its purpose, specific vocabulary (e.g., *minutes, seconds*), and their ability to follow the multistep procedures involved in reading a clock.

Student **interest** refers to whatever excites a student or evokes a particular cognitive, affective, social, or psychomotor connection. For example, a student might be interested in a particular topic (e.g., dinosaurs, music) or historical period (e.g., the Middle Ages, World War II).

Student **learning profile** is an umbrella term for the various aspects of a learner that create a more complete understanding of who that learner is as a unique and whole individual. It includes, but is not limited to, personal learning preferences, cultural foundation, gender, and sense of well-being. One student might prefer to work with others; another, to work alone. Still others might have a cultural background characteristic (e.g., fluency in another language) that orients their prior knowledge and comprehension of content in a particular way. Well-being is a vital aspect of a student's learning profile and includes numerous social-emotional learning skills (e.g., relationship skills, self-management, self-awareness, responsible decision making, social awareness).

When applying Tomlinson's differentiated instruction framework, educators make decisions based on their own setting and students rather than on a standardized way of doing things. They can expect to grow in their ability to practice differentiation and become more effective and successful over time. The model is applicable across different education settings, although the terminology remains the same; teachers thus both apply the concepts within their particular context and communicate in more general ways when collaborating with other practitioners. As with any conceptual model, the distinctions between categories sometimes oversimplify what might occur in a real setting. In practice, the four targets of differentiation and three dimensions of student variance will not always be distinct or isolated. For example, a teacher might find that a student's reading readiness can be affected by various aspects of their learning profile (e.g., low vision, adult support system they have at home, difficulty with emotional regulation, or cognitive delays).

A Reasoning Process for Designing Differentiated Instruction

Although there is a lot of flexibility in how teachers might differentiate a lesson, unit, or other learning experience, effective differentiation is the product of a reasoning process; it is not haphazard, random, or the result of a whim. DI offers freedom within a framework. What enables the creation of a learning experience that is dynamic and adjustable as well as consistently high quality is the disciplined reasoning process teachers exercise—one that allows their basic beliefs about learning, students, and educational options to be applied in practice.

We recommend focusing on five fundamental professional practices, some drawn directly from Tomlinson (2017a; 2017b): building on a foundation of high-quality curriculum, effectively using assessment to inform teaching and learning, providing respectful activities tailored to assessment-indicated student needs, employing strategic and flexible grouping, and considering students as collaborators in their own learning.

High-Quality Curriculum

A high-quality curriculum is clearly focused on the information and understandings that are most valued in a particular discipline. It incorporates learning experiences and outputs that are designed to ensure that students wrestle with, apply, and attain curriculum essentials as well as materials (including technologies) and tasks that are relevant to students. The curriculum involves students in learning across various domains (e.g., cognitive, affective, psychomotor) and promotes enjoyment and satisfaction in learning for each student.

Effective Use of Assessment

Assessment plays a crucial role in differentiation. Therefore, it is essential to use varied forms of both formative and summative assessment throughout the instructional cycle. For example, before instruction begins, a history teacher might explore what understanding students already have of ancient civilizations by giving them a short quiz (a pre-assessment) and then go on to design a unit that capitalizes on this existing knowledge.

Respectful Activities for All Students

Respect and care for all learners is foundational to differentiated instruction. It's an attitude that is incompatible with lowering expectations for some students for the purpose of having them experience "success." Instead, students receive the support they need to meet high expectations; teachers recognize that some students may require different types of learning experiences along the way to reach the goals set for the class.

When adjusting a lesson or assignment to make it a better fit for an individual student, one thing that is *not* adjusted is the quality of the learning experience and the engagement a student might find in it. For example, it would be inappropriate for one group of students to have an enjoyable, novel task while another group is expected to remediate. When differentiating, teachers strive to give every student access to learning that is meaningful and enriching.

Frequent Use of Flexible Grouping

Flexible grouping is the practice of putting students in a variety of learning configurations based on instructional goals. As these goals change, so does the group composition. For example, a teacher whose objective is to expand how students understand the concepts of *family* and *community* might use heterogeneous groups that consider students' cultures and prior experiences. Flexible grouping changes dynamically depending on instructional goals, allows students to understand how working together in groups supports their learning, and builds community and social skills. Teachers may assign students to groups or give students opportunities to create their own groups or pairs. According to Tomlinson (1995, 2014), using flexible and varied types of grouping allows students to see themselves in a variety of contexts and aids the educator in trying out various instructional grouping configurations to determine what works best for students.

Students and Teachers as Collaborators in the Learning Process

Although their roles are different, students and teachers in differentiated classrooms share responsibility for the success of learning. The role of students is to learn from and with their teachers and peers. They participate in ways that promote their own learning and that of others and are expected to gain new insights about themselves and make good choices to support their success through self-study. The role of teachers is to use their expertise to teach content, learn about their students, modify how students go about learning so they are more successful, and provide students with opportunities to learn about themselves. This includes teaching students how to make sense of their learning through self-reflection and analyzing their progress.

Why Should Teachers Differentiate Instruction?

Students are so obviously distinct and unique—why would we expect them to all learn the same way? If education is to be equitable and balance high expectations for all with a recognition of these differences, then there simply must be a regular practice of modifying instructional experiences to promote every student's optimal growth and learning. With the right desire and skill, every student can experience success. Differentiation just makes sense!

Research also confirms that differentiation is an effective method for supporting diverse learners. It is an approach that promotes meaningful instruction that is learner-, knowledge-, and assessment-centered—a kind of instruction that has been proven effective in supporting student learning (Bransford et al., 2000; Goddard et al., 2019).

Learner-centered environments are responsive to students' needs, culture, and interests; teachers "pay careful attention to the knowledge, skills, attitudes, and beliefs that learners bring to the educational setting" (Bransford et al., 2000, p. 133). **Knowledge-centered environments** focus on how students construct new knowledge by building on their prior knowledge, skills, and attitudes while also ensuring application and transfer of learning to new situations and promoting critical thinking and sense making. In **assessment-centered environments**, both teachers and students learn from the assessment process (i.e., pre-assessment, formative assessment, summative assessments). Clearly, students learn through effective assessment practices—and teachers learn, too. By examining and reflecting on assessment practices and results, teachers can modify and "rethink their teaching practices" (Bransford et al., 2000, p. 141).

A Design Orientation for Practicing Differentiation

One of the reasons for differentiated instruction's popularity is its emphasis on teacher professionalism, especially its recognition of a teacher's professional expertise—the skills and knowledge gained from formal education and through experience—and how this expertise is applied through instructional decisions that optimally benefit learners. Such professionalism and its application for serving others in practical contexts are things teachers share with those who work in a variety of fields: art, architecture, engineering, and more. In these fields, professionals who act as designers

- Work independently;
- Apply their specialized skills in real-world settings;
- Serve others by helping them achieve specific, important goals;
- Consult and collaborate with other design specialists;

- Engage the best and most powerful technologies available; and
- Continually expand their professional knowledge and expertise through reflection.

All teachers, especially those who aim to differentiate instruction, can benefit from thinking of themselves as design professionals. Embracing this concept allows you to connect with a community who shares your commitment to service through practice; borrow from their systematic, strategic ways of achieving goals; and adopt some of their methods. Approaching differentiation as an educational designer means you do not simply plan activities, deciding in advance which to implement and how to practically coordinate them. Instead, it means putting together an instructional plan that thoughtfully weighs different parameters (e.g., student characteristics, available time, materials) to determine the best way of achieving specific goals.

Thinking of themselves as educational designers can heighten teachers' awareness of the creative control they possess over many aspects of their work, including use of time, sequencing, grouping, and instructional materials. When teachers consciously relate their work to that of other design professionals, they tap into a mindset that is goal-centered and progressive, with heightened awareness of how practices used in other fields might be translated into educational practice (e.g., needs assessment, evaluation). In the sections that follow, we explain more about the benefits you can expect from thinking of yourself as an educational designer within a differentiated classroom. We also describe how functioning like a designer allows you to integrate technology more effectively as well as how more effective technology integration enables more effective differentiated practice. Although differentiation, design, and technology are distinct educational innovations and are often implemented separately, we propose they are best combined in a particular relationship and with a specific method.

What Makes Someone a Designer?

To understand what design is, it helps to analyze what designers do across different professional fields. Design professionals share common aspects that characterize their work, regardless of whether they function in interior, industrial, or educational design. Recognizing these common characteristics allows teachers to tap into the benefits derived from seeing themselves as part of a larger community of practical and valued experts, including rich guidance for how to go about their work (e.g., methods for goal setting, strategic planning, needs assessment).

Designers are client centered. They serve other people. Although an interior designer might serve a homeowner, an industrial designer might serve a business or a corporation, and an educational designer might serve a group of students, for each, the focus is on someone else.

Designers are goal oriented. They strive to achieve specific goals that are important to those they serve. An interior designer's goals relate to the client's need for a more functional and beautiful kitchen renovation. An industrial designer strives to increase production efficiency and lower manufacturing costs. An educational designer who wants to differentiate instruction aims to create the conditions required for students to master academic content, experience a sense of belonging, develop self-awareness, and gain independence.

Designers are strategic. A recognition of their goals and an awareness of the parameters that are important to consider in relation to them make it possible for designers to function with a strategy. The strategy is carefully developed to accomplish identified goals in the "best" way after recognizing various possibilities exist. This might mean moving forward in a more cost- or time-effective way or in a way that requires less energy or avoids unnecessary difficulties.

Designers possess specialized knowledge and skills. Regardless of the field, designers know things that equip them for their work. An interior designer understands color, space, and light and has project management skills. An industrial designer appreciates the details of product development, sustainability, and human-centered design. Educational designers in a differentiated classroom comprehend the elements of instruction under their control and understand how to adjust them based on the readiness, interests, and learning profiles of their students.

Designers deploy powerful technology in strategic ways. The degree of thoughtfulness and intention that characterizes other aspects of a designer's work also influences this one. Designers identify the technologies that will have the most benefit for the potential costs and drawbacks (e.g., requirement of expertise for operating them, potential for malfunction).

Designers grow in their expertise over time and with experience. They become more efficient and effective in their work as they engage in and reflect on their professional experiences. As a result, they are increasingly valued for their advanced knowledge that is only possible from engaging in the risks of learning in a real-world setting.

How Can Teachers Who Differentiate Adopt a Design Orientation?

Teachers who approach their work with a design orientation, as educational designers, adopt a particular mindset, skill set, and tool set (Kilbane & Milman, 2014). Each of these is distinctly helpful, and all combine to enhance the sophistication and effectiveness of the various aspects of teaching practice. By adopting a design **mindset**—a deliberate way of thinking about their work—teachers approach decision making more strategically and systematically (e.g., how to balance students' individual and shared needs) because they have guidance when identifying goals and understanding how best to achieve them. By developing a designer's **skill set**, teachers acquire a collection of key practices (e.g., flexible grouping, learning contracts) and professional competencies (e.g., analysis, reflection) that can be implemented to enable each student to succeed. Using this skill set, in turn, opens up additional opportunities to learn from experience and expedites the development of professional expertise. By acquiring a powerful **tool set**—expert knowledge of and proficiency with the instructional models, strategies, and technologies—teachers can respond to their students' needs more flexibly and appropriately. This tool set expands the options they have available to support the design and delivery of instruction and helps them address some of the challenges associated with frequent, consistent differentiated instruction. A design orientation gives educators what they need to understand their students, adapt instruction for their benefit, and coordinate the many resources available for teaching in contemporary classrooms.

Using Digital Tools to Support Differentiated Instruction

As we have explained, functioning as an educational designer is not just compatible with differentiation but instrumental for its effective implementation, especially given the innumerable possibilities for teaching in a post-pandemic profession. What, then, should educational technology, or *digital tools,* achieve for the educational designer who strives to differentiate instruction?

The integration of technology in any education setting should always make learning more equitable, efficient, effective, and engaging—in other words, it should accomplish the *4Es* (Kilbane & Milman, 2023). The incorporation of digital tools should provide equitable access to learning for all students, as well as save time (one way of addressing efficiency). For example, using a learning management system (e.g., Blackboard, Canvas, Moodle, Schoology) makes it quicker for students to access the materials their teacher allows them to choose from based on their readiness when completing an activity. Technology integration should also result in more successful learning (one way of making learning more effective), such as when incorporating an animated graphic while presenting academic content results in students' deeper conceptual understanding of a scientific process. In addition, it should boost students' interest in and enjoyment of learning, such as when students are encouraged to choose from a range of digital tools that inspire them to invest more energy in completing assignments. As these examples suggest, the 4Es provide helpful guidance for teachers in any education setting to address their specific goals for differentiation. The 4Es can also be used as a rubric of sorts, allowing teachers to consider both whether and how technology might add value to a learning experience. We'll delve more deeply into the 4Es in Chapter 2.

Describing these goals of technology integration for educational designers who differentiate instruction identifies what digital tools should help achieve, but it doesn't illuminate their full influence on education. Although the integration of digital tools has great promise for supporting the goals of differentiation, it is not without risks and drawbacks. The very same technologies that can enhance, expedite, or expand learning can also compromise it. For instance, the use of artificial intelligence (AI) technology can aid student learning or impede it, depending on why it's being used, the skills students are being asked to employ, and the quality or accuracy of the information that AI generates. One student might use AI to facilitate brainstorming, and another, to cheat. One student might be skilled at prompting (i.e., asking questions of) the AI tool, and another, with less skill, might become overwhelmed or confused by the information output of the AI tool.

The same technologies that aid one student can be detrimental to others who lack the conditions for their effective use. In this book, we address the specific ways that you can carefully consider the benefits of technology while also identifying challenges it may present to differentiating the classroom community (Chapter 3), the content of learning (Chapter 6), the learning process (Chapter 7), and more. To implement digital tools optimally, all designers—especially educational designers—must understand the relationship of technology to design and to their work as designers, as well as ensure careful consideration of technology's affordances, challenges, and potential for harm.

Before digging deeper into these concepts, it is important to clarify certain terminology. First, we use the term *technology* as it is commonly used in the field of education: to refer to a specific class of digital or electronic tools. Second, our use of this term refers to a wide variety of hardware (e.g., devices like computers, calculators, tablets, clickers), applications (e.g., software, apps, websites), and environments (e.g., virtual spaces like Zoom breakout rooms, discussion boards) that support the activities of education.

The Relationship Between Technology and Design

Human beings have had a long and interesting relationship with different tools across history. Archimedes, the ancient Greek mathematician, inventor, and engineer, was particularly fond of levers, an important mechanical advancement of his era. His assertion "Give me a lever and a place to stand and I can move the Earth" has been repeated by leaders through the ages to emphasize the power of tools and technology. But this quote also conveys an additional, complicated truth: A tool can be powerful but still insufficient for a job. And there is no tool—simple or complex, mechanical or electronic, inexpensive or costly—that can achieve its purpose if the conditions for use aren't an appropriate fit. One of the most important conditions determining the efficacy of any tool is its user; simply put, the user needs to know how to make the best use of the tool.

The principles of differentiation and high-quality instructional design for achieving them are the crucial foundation for the effective use of any digital tools. With this "place to stand," teachers who function as educational designers can employ digital tools in more strategic, balanced, and powerful ways. A teacher's ability to design for differentiation is the firm footing that allows them to integrate differentiation strategies and technology in ways that are both meaningful and successful. This is why technology, although an important aspect of this book, is not its primary focus. Both technology in general and distinct digital tools in particular aid teachers and students in the various aspects of their differentiated learning. Differentiation can be achieved through the application of a design mindset and skill set. The tool set, which includes digital tools, relies on the successful application of the other two.

Although technology has the power to aid differentiated practice in varied ways—from planning to lesson implementation, evaluation, and more—technology is valuable only to the degree that it supports the goals of differentiated instruction, the work of the teacher in achieving these goals, and the success of every learner. This might mean that teachers use digital tools to adjust content, process, product, and environment. It might also mean they take advantage of various technologies to address barriers that prevent their more frequent and powerful efforts to differentiate. What is distinct about an educational designer's use of such tools is that a particular tool is carefully selected and used for an intended purpose and with a certain goal in mind. This thoughtful incorporation allows an educational designer to evaluate the tool's effect (i.e., whether it was beneficial) based on the degree to which it helped achieve its intended purpose. The tools selected will vary by grade level, content area, and learning goal. For example, a social studies teacher might choose a spreadsheet for students to create and conduct data analysis of primary source information they have collected to learn about a period of time for a community in a particular part of the world. Then the teacher would evaluate the effectiveness of the tool in helping them analyze the data and come to conclusions about it.

Today's digital tools are more diverse and complex than the simple tools of Archimedes's time. There is a big difference between a lever and a smartphone! Recognizing that even digital technologies we might think of as belonging to the same class or category (e.g., graphic design tools such as Adobe Spark and Canva) are distinct and can be profoundly different from one another is an essential understanding for educational designers. Each digital tool has its own effect on people (e.g., amplifies or augments what they can achieve unaided, and, in some cases, even hinders achievement) and the environment (e.g., expands the time and space for learning). Likewise, the method of implementing a specific digital tool has different effects on people (e.g., enabling them to relate more, or less, to others) and the environment (e.g., making it more, or less, conducive for certain activities). The tools that are determined to be "most appropriate" will necessarily vary based on context, including the grade level, subject area, and particular goals for the tools' use.

Adopting a design orientation influences how teachers approach their work; it also has a particularly strong effect on how they leverage the tools available to them. This seemingly simple competency—the effective application of technology—makes a tremendous difference in every aspect of differentiated instruction, including teachers' conceptualization of learning design, its implementation, and ways for evaluating its effects. Teachers functioning as educational designers will not only find it easier to develop proficiency with digital tools (e.g., operating them effectively and with precision) but also be equipped to understand why this proficiency might be helpful (e.g., understanding when a tool can make a real difference) and when it is most meaningfully applied (e.g., to free up time for more enriching interpersonal interactions). They will especially appreciate that the value of a tool lies not in itself but in what it does to help them achieve the specific, important, and pre-established goals tied to the success of every one of their students.

Approaching Differentiation as a Designer

Tomlinson's 1995 publication about differentiated instruction was innovative in many ways. Perhaps most important, it reflected a pronounced shift in the perception of the educator's role. Tomlinson encourages teachers to recognize their power and talents, embrace their position as instructional decision makers, and be more fully what they already were: creative, professional advocates for their students. Without explicitly saying so, she encourages teachers to function as designers who methodically address the diverse needs of their unique learners rather than being inflexible instructors who aim for the middle and offer one-size-fits-all instruction. This view is consistent with approaching teaching with a design mindset and is one of the hallmarks of our book.

Over time and with deliberate application, teachers who differentiate instruction and approach it as educational designers will become increasingly adept at employing a vast array of methods, resources, and technologies to transform their students' learning experiences and lives. Working as an educational designer will make it easier for you to identify your students' unique needs, develop the most appropriate learning outcomes for them, and apply your professional expertise to address barriers that impede each student's optimal growth. It will allow you to transform your classroom—whether physical, virtual, or some combination of the two—into a productive, functional learning environment and give you greater professional freedom and increased satisfaction. It will enable you to use a variety of tools, many of which will involve digital technology, and teach in a way that not only celebrates but also fully accommodates the unique students you serve.

Questions for Reflection

- Reflect on your role as a teacher. How do you use differentiated instruction in your practice?
- What are a few ways you might more effectively incorporate differentiation and technology into your teaching practice?
- What is your educational philosophy, and how is it reflected in your use of differentiation?
- Do you approach your work as an educational designer? How might you increase the intent, regularity, and power with which you design instruction with an educational designer's mindset, skill set, and tool set?

2

Selecting Digital Tools to Support Differentiated Instruction

This chapter covers...

- The benefits of integrating digital tools into instructional practice.
- The types of technology knowledge and supports that are best suited for a differentiated classroom.
- Ways to ensure digital tool use will support the goals of differentiation.

The right tool can be transformational in the hands of a carpenter, a sculptor, or an educator. It can save time and effort, improve the quality of work, and even make a task more enjoyable. However, these benefits come only when a tool is used properly by someone with the necessary skills and knowledge. A lot of the ed tech now common in classrooms offers great promise for assisting with various aspects of high-quality instruction. However, the sheer number, wide variety, and great complexity of digital tools make it challenging to know when to use them, how best to use them, and whether they have a positive, justifiable influence on reaching the goals of differentiation.

Deciding the most appropriate and powerful way to integrate technology requires **technological pedagogical content knowledge**, or **"TPACK"** (Mishra & Koehler, 2006). TPACK is a concept that expands on Shulman's (1986, 1987) concept of pedagogical content knowledge (also referred to as PCK), which is a type of unique teacher professional knowledge involving teachers' knowledge of pedagogy coupled with knowledge of their content area (i.e., content knowledge, or CK ; for more about CK, see Chapter 6). TPACK adds technology to the acronym. It "requires a foundational knowledge in all teaching domains," "a specialized knowledge of their integration," and "knowing when and when not to use technology to support teaching and learning in the content areas, as well as how to do so most effectively" (Kilbane & Milman, 2014, p. 50). Teachers are constantly developing and applying TPACK when they use and integrate technology in their teaching. Figure 2.1 provides a visual representation of TPACK.

FIGURE 2.1
The Technological Pedagogical Content Knowledge (TPACK) Model

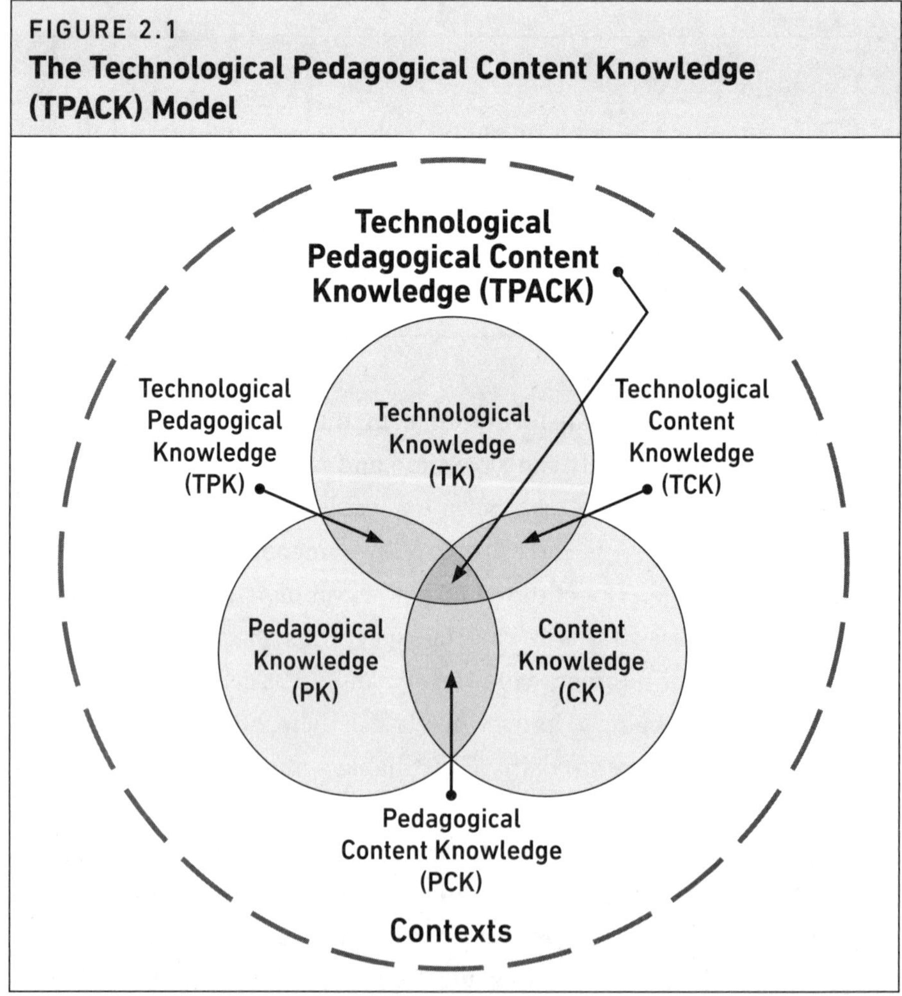

Copyright © 2012 by TPACK.org. Reproduced with permission.

What Are Digital Tools?

Consider how different a graphing calculator, a cloud-based spreadsheet, and a smartphone are from one another. Each performs different functions, requires certain skills from the user, and costs a different amount of money. One of these tools relies on electricity alone, whereas the others require a connection to a communication network. There are innumerable features that distinguish one digital tool from another and influence their usability and appropriateness for different contexts and tasks.

In educational settings, it's common to categorize digital tools by the primary role they play in the teaching–learning process: as (1) administrative technologies, (2) operational technologies, or (3) pedagogical technologies. There is some overlap here; a tool might fit into two or more categories based on its functions (e.g., a smartphone is both a communication device and a calculator) or method of implementation (e.g., a spreadsheet could support learning or record keeping). Tools in each of these categories—many of them open source or free—have great promise for positively influencing learning in differentiated classrooms.

Administrative Technologies

Teachers use administrative technologies for recordkeeping and communicating, gaining support that helps them carry out their many responsibilities while streamlining tasks and improving efficiency. They use apps or software to record attendance and grades, share progress reports with students and families, create newsletters, or generate email and other communications to keep their classroom community up to date. In differentiated classrooms, administrative technology can also support the construction of a learning community (more on this in Chapter 3).

Operational Technologies

Operational technologies—apps, software, and online tools—assist teachers and students with planning, organizing, and managing activities associated with learning. These tools can help

- Expedite lesson planning (e.g., lesson planning wizards, repositories);
- Schedule spaces, resources, and meetings;

- Organize materials (often called "provisioning");
- Create assessments, rubrics, and surveys; and
- Manage student groups and assignments.

Operational technologies can save teachers time—time that can be reallocated to activities in support of differentiation (e.g., conferencing with students, designing pre-assessments, creating more sophisticated learning experiences). Wisely selected operational technologies also remove some of the logistical challenges associated with differentiation, making it easier, for example, to keep track of resources and analyze data to determine the best methods of grouping for particular assignments or tasks.

Pedagogical Technologies

Pedagogical technologies are digital tools used to support activities necessary to meet the learning goals within a particular setting (e.g., an online-only 12th grade government class in Ohio, a 5th grade hybrid science classroom in Oregon, a kindergarten classroom in Nevada). These technologies support students' exploration of concepts (e.g., simulations, 3D modeling), knowledge construction (e.g., concept mapping, matrices, hypermedia), articulation and expression (e.g., multimedia, presentation tools), reflection (e.g., annotation, screencasting), and social learning (e.g., videoconferencing, discussions). Tools in the pedagogical technology category help teachers do some of the core work of differentiation, including varying the environment, content, process, and products associated with learning.

Pedagogical technologies are more varied than administrative or operational ones; they operate as extensions of a teacher's educational philosophy and conception of learning, even when that philosophy may not be a consciously held set of beliefs. For example, if you're a teacher with a traditional (i.e., objectivist) approach to teaching, you might use presentation tools, images, or videos to streamline how you introduce content. If you favor a more contemporary (i.e., constructivist) approach, you likely use tools such as spreadsheets, databases, graphic organizers, or multimedia to help you manipulate data or compare and contrast, supporting your students' construction of knowledge (e.g., new concepts and ideas they develop themselves). David Jonassen, an early and important scholar of educational technology, recognized the ways that different technologies act in the design for learning. He explained that students can both "learn from" and "learn with" digital tools (1996).

The SAMR model, developed by researcher Ruben Puentedura (2013), expands on Jonassen's ideas about how technology supports student-centered learning. It also carries forward the insight of Fulton and Reil (1999), who noted that "technology allows one to do things differently, and to do different things" (para. 1). SAMR stands for *substitution, augmentation, modification,* and *redefinition,* and the SAMR model classifies classroom technology integration into these four categories—two that enhance traditional learning activities and two that transform traditional activities into something new:

- **Substitution** means using a digital tool as a direct substitute for an analog one with no functional difference in how students take in or process information. An example would be an art teacher displaying images of Monet's *Water Lilies* series of paintings on a screen via a digital projector (rather than displaying printed posters) while describing features of the works.
- **Augmentation** means using a digital tool as a direct substitute for an analog one in a way that results in a positive functional change (an enhancement) in how students perceive it. For example, the art teacher mentioned might decide to use an interactive whiteboard to write on or mark up digital images of paintings in Monet's *Water Lilies* series while modeling how to critique this artwork so that students can clearly see how the critique relates to the paintings' features.
- **Modification** means using a digital tool to rework or redesign a task in order to promote and meet a new learning goal. An example of modification might be the art teacher's students using VoiceThread, an interactive multimedia discussion tool. Students look at digital images of paintings in Monet's *Water Lilies* series; add digital markup; and post their own text, audio, or video critique of the works.
- **Redefinition** means using digital tools to interact with the content in an entirely new way. For example, to demonstrate their understanding of Monet's Impressionism, students might use an augmented

reality (AR) app to design their own artwork to be viewed and experienced in the physical world through the AR app on a smartphone or tablet. Other students would then provide feedback, using the same AR tools to show their own knowledge and ability to critique their peer's artwork and analytical contributions.

The Bloom's digital taxonomy, developed by Andrew Churches (2008), is another popular model that can help teachers assess digital pedagogical tools and decide which will benefit their students—and when. Built on the revised Bloom's taxonomy (Anderson et al., 2001), a hierarchy that distinguishes between different types of cognitive activities, Churches's model illustrates how digital tools and activities can support or reflect different types of thinking. For example, the revised Bloom's taxonomy lists six key terms relating to thinking skills, among them *creating* and *analyzing*. The digital Bloom's taxonomy identifies technology-driven or technology-supported activities associated with each thinking skill. So, for example, programming, filming, animating, blogging/vlogging, wiki-ing, and podcasting are examples of activities that involve creating (or creative thinking), and mashing, linking, reverse engineering, and hacking are examples of activities that involve analyzing (or analytical thinking). Others have taken this model and run with it. For example, on her *Kaffeeklatsch* blog, educational technology specialist Kathy Schrock (2024) lists apps, online tools, and Google Workspace apps by Bloom's taxonomy category and provides a diagram illustrating how the SAMR model relates to the taxonomy.

We want the information in this chapter and throughout this book to empower teachers to make their own decisions about when, if, and how to incorporate digital tools in their practice. We recognize that while teachers who differentiate share common beliefs about the importance of serving all learners, they also differ in countless ways. They may choose different tools to best serve their learners within their specific environment. Professional discretion is necessary to differentiate appropriately. Indeed, a hallmark of differentiated instruction is the intentional way that teachers plan instruction, and teachers need this same kind of intention when planning how they will integrate the technologies they and their students will use. When designing a differentiated lesson plan, including one that integrates technology, it helps to adopt the right mindset and follow guidance on key practices.

Selecting the Right Digital Tools

There are many factors to consider when choosing which digital tools to incorporate, especially the pedagogical ones that will support teaching and learning.

First, can the tool be used in a way that supports students as they work to master the learning goals? And how can technology support both the learning goals and differentiated instruction? Which technology, if any, should be used and for what differentiated purposes? Is the technology being used to substitute, augment, modify, or redefine the learning goals in some way? If so, how?

After making this determination, teachers need to address other factors related to the technology under consideration—specifically its **affordances and constraints**. *Affordance* refers to the range of positive possibilities or outcomes associated with the implementation of a digital tool; *constraints* include the many and varied drawbacks or negative possibilities associated with the implementation of a digital tool. For example, one affordance of allowing students to use a multimedia tool when creating a culminating assignment at the end of a unit (a product) is that it opens up a variety of ways for them to express what they have learned, increasing motivation and student expression. One constraint, though, is that students might need more time to design and assemble a digital presentation than they would to share their learning in a traditional written report or oral presentation. Another constraint would be the risk of students getting distracted or sidetracked by the digital tool's fancy features and failing to accurately present the breadth and depth of their learning.

Affordances and constraints must be weighed carefully in differentiated settings where teachers have clear goals, a strategy, and an expansive understanding of their students. Which students might benefit? Which might struggle? What might those struggles look like? These considerations should factor into the decision of whether to incorporate a digital tool and should inform the design of learning experiences overall. In addition to thinking critically about a tool's affordances and constraints, it is helpful to apply other criteria to the selection of any category of digital tools but especially when considering pedagogical ones (see Figure 2.2).

FIGURE 2.2
Considerations for Selecting Digital Tools

Criteria	Considerations
Cost and access	• Is it free? If not, how much does it cost? Is there a one-time cost or subscription? How will I finance purchasing this tool? • If the digital tool is to be used at home, will all my students be able to access it?
Data privacy	• Will students' data be properly protected using this digital tool? • Do students have permission to use it? • Does this digital tool fit the school's acceptable use policy? • How are students' data used? Can students and parents or guardians opt out of data mining?
Classification	• What type of technology is this—administrative, operational, or pedagogical? • Is it a physical device, installed software or app, cloud-based application, or a combination? • Do I already have access to other tools in this classification? If so, how is this one distinct?
Reliability	• How likely is it that this digital tool will break? • How likely is it that this digital tool will not work or malfunction?
Uses	• What was the tool designed to do? Are there other ways it can be used? • How does this tool influence teaching and learning in this context? —What are the positive effects? —Will it promote equitable opportunities for learning? —Will it be helpful to students who might need its assistance? —Are there any negative effects? —Will using this tool make learning more difficult or problematic for some students? • In what ways will it make learning more efficient, effective, and engaging for some or all students?

Criteria	Considerations
Versatility	• How many different contexts are there for this digital tool to be helpful? • Can students use the tool in different ways? • Will the tool accommodate low- and high-tech expression of student learning?
Ease of use	• How difficult or easy is it to use this digital tool? What type of skills and knowledge are required? • Do all students possess the needed skills or knowledge? • Will the use be equitable—will all students be able to use it?
Degree of dependence	• How many integrated technologies (e.g., a tablet needs both the internet and apps) are involved in the full and successful use of this digital tool? • Are all of these technologies available to support the successful use of this tool?
Technology support	• What type of support is available to help users with the digital tool (online tutorials, live chat, email)?
Engagement	• Will students like using this digital tool? Will it add motivation and enjoyment to the learning task? • Will this digital tool serve as too great a distraction from other aspects of learning?

Choosing Technology to Cultivate Equitable, Efficient, Effective, and Engaging Differentiated Instruction

Asking yourself whether implementation of a digital tool will make learning more *equitable, efficient, effective,* and *engaging* can improve all aspects of your work–administrative, operational, and pedagogical. Using these "4Es" (Kilbane & Milman, 2014; 2023) as an informal decision-making rubric promotes both the broad goal of differentiation (i.e., providing optimal support to promote the success of all learners) and more discrete and practical goals like fitting in a specific lesson before lunch or keeping students interested in a topic long enough to achieve mastery.

Let's take a moment to look more closely at each of the 4Es and the ways in which technology can be used and integrated to make differentiated instruction more equitable, efficient, effective, and engaging.

Equitable Instruction

Different students need different types of support if they are to achieve success. Thus, for educational experiences to be equitable, every student must receive what they need to succeed—even when this means that some students will get more support in comparison to their peers.

Teachers who differentiate instruction strive to make individualized support a reality and to create communities where students and parents understand and value this approach. In most educational settings, digital tools are already employed as part of efforts to make learning experiences more equitable. Examples include permitting students in a physics class to use calculators or setting up digital reading material so that students can click on important vocabulary words and find definitions and illustrations to supplement comprehension. Teachers adept at differentiation also understand that many students will benefit from the routine incorporation of accommodations originally designed to help students overcome deficits (e.g., graphic organizers, explicit instruction, segmenting learning tasks).

Any plans for integrating technology in a differentiated classroom should take into consideration affordances and constraints, focus on addressing the goals of differentiation, and also respond to the "5As" addressing equity and access (Roberts & Hernandez, 2019):

1. **Availability.** Is the technology available to all? During learning? At home?
2. **Affordability.** Is the technology affordable for all for use outside school?
3. **Awareness.** Are students equally knowledgeable of how this technology can assist them if they are able to access it?
4. **Abilities.** Do all students have the digital literacies and other capabilities (e.g., physical, intellectual) to use this technology?
5. **Agency.** Do all students have the self-efficacy to make use of the technology? During learning? At home?

Efficient Instruction

To recognize a practice as "efficient" means noting the ways in which it preserves resources—including time, effort, and money, in any combination—without sacrificing output quality. Integrating digital tools into instructional practice presents many opportunities for improved efficiency. For example, you might gain instructional time by tailoring multimedia materials created for the whole class to target specific learner needs. Students might work more effortlessly and use their time more wisely when they are able to access an organized selection of research materials via a website you've created. You might save your department money when you use free online services to create powerful learning opportunities.

One of the least considered and most promising aspects of efficiency that digital tools can contribute to overlaps with promoting more effective practice—that is, when teachers use digital tools in a way that not only frees up time, energy, or resources but also reallocates these factors in ways that enhance learning. Time that would have been spent on administrative or repetitive tasks, such as handing out papers or delivering the same 15-minute lecture to four different sections of World History I, can be spent instead on tasks that have a greater effect, such as recording a video lecture that students can watch and rewatch at home, reteaching content as needed in targeted groups, delivering individualized feedback, or using generative AI prompts to quickly come up with calculation problems linked to specific areas of student interest—whether that's aeronautics, ballet, or any number of subjects. The increased efficiency technology offers is one of its greatest strengths—one that gives educational designers opportunities to redirect time and effort toward the kind of personalization, connection, and feedback that nurtures people, builds relationships, and supports joyful learning.

Effective Instruction

Effective instruction is that which enables the greatest number of learners to meet its targeted learning goals. Success can be measured through improved learning outcomes for individuals or the whole class. More effective instruction might also be that which results in greater amounts of learning, deeper learning, or learning that is more rewarding for both students and teacher. Examples of digital tools employed to support effective instruction abound.

Take, for example, the use of digital texts and text-to-speech by students with dyslexia or low vision. Both technologies provide these students equitable access to critical ideas and content. Or consider the use of visualization tools (e.g., diagrams, charts, animations); by depicting abstract ideas or diffuse data sets in more concrete ways, these can make content more comprehensible for any student who is struggling with it.

Engaging Instruction

Tools that evoke cognitive, affective, and psychomotor interest make learning more engaging. Many digital tools that are familiar and useful to students outside school, such as the phones and tablets they use to text, take photos, and make videos, can and should be incorporated into schoolwork. These familiar tools can lower the barrier to task entry and even help students see that "school life" and "real life" are not so far apart. When teachers infuse technology use into educational design to make the learning experience more novel, entertaining, and sensory rich, they boost both student attention and motivation (Harper & Milman, 2016; Milman et al., 2014). For example, simply using audience response systems, clickers, or text-based polling can increase engagement. Interactive tools have the power to transform even the most mundane learning experiences—improving students' focus, piquing curiosity, and increasing enjoyment in the learning process.

Using Digital Tools to Transform Challenges into Opportunities

The 4Es provide helpful guidance for all teachers and additional assistance to those differentiating instruction. Teachers can identify the barriers to implementing certain differentiated practices more frequently or effectively, then consider how incorporating technology might transform would-be barriers into opportunities for even greater success. In Figure 2.3, you'll find some examples of how digital tools can support differentiated practices by making learning more equitable, efficient, effective, and engaging in one or more ways.

FIGURE 2.3

How Digital Tool Application Can Support and Transform Differentiation

Practice	Barrier	Digital Tool Application	Transformation
Regular pre-assessment	Time-consuming to distribute, review, and analyze data	Online pre-assessment saves time for distribution; it organizes and displays data, facilitating analysis.	Pre-assessment is more frequently and powerfully practiced. More accurate and timely data cultivate more data-informed differentiation.
Working with groups of students at different levels of readiness	Difficult for the teacher to work with more than one group at a time	Pre-recorded presentation of content for different groups "frees up" the teacher to work with individuals or groups.	Personalized guidance and interaction provide just-in-time support to the students who need it most.
Regular formative assessment	Generates more content for a teacher to review	Students annotate their own work with digital tools built into apps or create think-aloud videos that describe what they did and learned.	Students benefit from developing their ability to self-critique; teacher energy otherwise spent providing feedback can be focused elsewhere. Teachers also have a deeper understand of what their students learned.
Individualized instructions	Tedious; takes energy and time to individualize	Teacher records instructions in audio or video files while writing the lesson plan; the instructions are accessible on shared documents assigned to different students. Teachers use AI to generate individualized instructions for students.	Students get the support they need; with minimal effort, the teacher can extend greater support for other students as well. Teachers can personalize instructions and reuse or revise them for other students.

(continued)

FIGURE 2.3—*(continued)*

How Digital Tool Application Can Support and Transform Differentiation

Practice	Barrier	Digital Tool Application	Transformation
Offering students choice in how they learn and demonstrate their learning	Difficulty anticipating students' choices and assembling materials and resources in advance and also teaching students how to use the tools effectively	Students can choose different multimedia (e.g., slide presentation, podcast, video), virtual reality, or augmented reality tools to develop and share/present their final products.	Teacher effort to provision materials is minimized and students gain greater agency, creativity, and choice.
Documenting student work in progress	Time-consuming to capture various stages of progress and keep it all organized	Students make their own videos and/or save and share different versions of their work online or in a digital folder.	Teachers use their time more efficiently which allows them to concentrate on those students who most need their support. Students become responsible for their own work and learn to track their progress across the learning progression. Teachers can evaluate learning over time.
Peer feedback to create a learning community	Logistically challenging and time-consuming and can also result in incorrect information	Students share digital materials on a collaborative website, then provide comments and feedback during or after school.	Limited time in the physical classroom is offset by expanding virtual spaces for learning.

The way to become a more skilled integrator of digital tools is by employing key practices that support high-quality instruction across grade-level, subject-area, and other contextual factors. These include

- Focusing on learning goals and objectives independent of the technology components;
- Planning for success by planning for technology failure;
- Establishing classroom and technology management procedures;
- Practicing with digital tools;
- Building in time to experiment with digital tools; and
- Reflecting on tech-integration experiences to learn from them.

Focus on Learning Goals and Objectives

Clearly, the 5As and 4Es are essential to consider when designing tech-infused differentiated instruction—but so are goals, objectives, and learning standards. Learning goals and objectives might need to include development and refinement of a variety of skills that technology can also support. For example, when asking students to analyze data about a subject they are learning (e.g., average sea-level temperatures for the past 100 years around the world), they need to have or develop data analysis skills using spreadsheet software.

Plan for Success by Planning for Failure

Ask not *if* technical problems will occur in your classroom but rather *when*. Regardless of a teacher's skill level with software, hardware, and troubleshooting, that teacher will benefit from planning with the aim of minimizing wasted time, distracted students, and other instructional challenges. Two types of planning should be used for every effort to integrate technology: a proactive plan and a reactive plan.

A **proactive plan** is made in advance to minimize the risk of something going awry. A **reactive plan** is what you will do if technical difficulties occur despite your proactive efforts. No matter how well you plan, it is likely you will need to troubleshoot at least some technical issues.

Take, for example, a 50-minute computer lab for a class of 7th graders. The students might take five minutes to settle into their seats in the lab when they first arrive. Then, they will need time to log into the network, launch the software, enter their passwords, and begin working on the learning activity. Factoring in time to log out and clean up the lab, the students will have approximately 30 minutes to complete the lesson. Given these time constraints, you'll need to put plans in place to maximize academic learning time. How do you do that?

First, brainstorm the potential difficulties related to technology and otherwise, such as computers or software not working, students not having the technical skills to work independently, or students finishing early or needing additional help. Next, develop a proactive plan that addresses those potential difficulties. Figure 2.4 provides some examples of difficulties and plans.

But wait—you're not done! You also need to develop a reactive plan to help you troubleshoot, which might look something like this:

- If there is a **minor problem** that can be fixed during class time, contact the technology coordinator for help and use the remaining time for work. While the technology coordinator is working to solve the problem, make use of learning time by asking students to use pencil and paper to begin their work. Prepare them to transfer this work to the computer when the problem is resolved.
- If there is a **major problem**, proceed with plans for the next activity in the unit. Contact the technology coordinator about the problem and reserve the computer lab for the following day.

Establish Classroom and Technology Management Procedures

Harry K. Wong, an extraordinary educator and professional development expert, pointed out that classroom procedures are more useful and important than rules (Wong & Wong, 2018). After all, if a classroom lacks standard operating procedures, disruption and disorder can easily get in the way of learning. Teachers who successfully differentiate instruction usually have established many procedures to ensure the smooth execution of their assessments, lessons, and classroom management practices. Those who incorporate technology must include even more. Some general procedures that apply to all environments where technology will be used include the following:

FIGURE 2.4

Potential Technology Integration Difficulties and Plans to Resolve Them

Potential Difficulty	Possible Plan
The computers, software, or network are not working, or there aren't enough tools for students to work independently.	Ensure the computers are in full functioning condition beforehand, with network or web access, software loaded properly, and so on. Check during your free period and send a note to the tech coordinator in advance asking them to check as well. Find out where the coordinator will be during the lesson in case problems crop up. Have a backup plan and use it if hardware, software, or the internet fails to work. It may also be helpful to have a backup plan if an individual student, a small group, or the whole class struggles to use a certain tool.
Students do not have their log-in information, or their log-in does not work.	Remind students to keep track of their network log-ins. Have them regularly check their log-in information on your classroom computer to make sure they remember it and know if it is still working. Ask them to write down this information (or determine a way to remember it) on their assignment sheet or store it in a note on their smartphone.
Students are not sure what the learning activity goals and standards are, or they waste time getting to the task.	Describe the assigned tasks and intended objectives to students prior to the lesson. Make sure that students' questions are answered and that they have a hard copy of the assignment instructions so that they can refer back to the process.
Students don't have the technical skills necessary to work independently.	Schedule parent volunteers, school "tech team" members, or peer experts to assist students who may need extra help.
Students finish the task early.	Remind students of the procedures for what to do if they finish the task early, such as "work on free-choice computer activities."
Something unanticipated happens to foil one or more students' efforts with the task.	Remind students of your standard operating procedures, such as "make eye contact with the teacher to indicate a need for help," and "ask peers for help."

- Turning devices on and off;
- Accessing required resources;
- Asking for help;
- Solving technical problems (e.g., a frozen screen, a jammed printer);
- Retrieving forgotten log-ins and passwords;
- Addressing inappropriate content;
- Dealing with bullying (e.g., a harassing email or instant message from another student);
- A broken hyperlink in an assignment;
- Saving work (e.g., on the file server) and naming files;
- Retrieving erased or lost work;
- Backing up/saving work; and
- Submitting completed assignments

It's also a good idea to develop procedures students can follow when working with technology outside school hours. What should students do if the technology isn't working, they can't access the internet, or they're otherwise unable to complete the assigned work?

Build in Time to Assess Access and to Provide Practice and Experimentation with Digital Tools

When technology use is part of a learning activity, teachers need to ensure all of their students have access to the technology resources they need in school and at home. They must also determine if the students (and family members, if applicable) have the knowledge and skills to use them as intended.

Similarly, when implementing a new technology, it is good practice to test out the tool using student equipment and interfaces to ensure that it works. Do a trial or practice run of any tools you plan to use with students, especially if these tools are new to you, to them, or to the school; it will help you prepare for the worst and expect the best. Often technology seems to work just fine on one's own computer but then there may be some "work-arounds" required or other challenges when using them on students' computers or on a larger scale. By doing a practice run with the technology, you can identify where challenges might arise and be prepared for them—or create materials to help students use the digital tools.

As any kindergarten teacher knows, before students can *learn* from manipulatives, they first need time to *play* with them. Play fulfills a human need to explore and work out the excitement of new experiences. Students—whether they are age 5 or age 15—benefit from time to experiment, play, and practice with new technology. Provide this time, either inside or outside class time, before expecting students to do anything meaningful with the technology.

One way to make exploration with new technologies during class time purposeful is to give students time to play and then have them showcase a feature of the tool or a tip or trick for their classmates. Students benefit from teaching one another, and the demonstrations let the teacher know how proficient students are with the tool and what supports might be needed to ensure that everyone can use the tool equitably and effectively. Another strategy is to pair use of the new tool with a community-building activity by asking students to share information about themselves using the new tool.

These strategies benefit the class individually and collectively and work in all grade levels and education settings. Once students have worked out the kinks of a new digital tool and gotten their excitement under control, they will gain more out of instructional learning time provided for its application.

Reflect to Learn from Experience

The final key practice that supports successful differentiation with technology is reflecting on successes and failures. As John Dewey observed, "we do not learn from experience, but from reflecting on experience" (1933, p. 78). Disciplined reflection turns memory into professional knowledge. Here are some questions to consider:

- What did students learn?
- What evidence is there of their learning?
- Was what students learned what you *intended* for them to learn?
- Did all students learn? If not, what might have been done to better support those who did not learn?
- Was the lesson design appropriate? How could it have been improved?

- Was the lesson implementation effective? How is effectiveness determined? What evidence is there?
- What was learned from this experience that will be useful in future planning with differentiated instruction/technology?

You don't need to reflect on all lessons—just the ones you want to learn from. Using these questions can turn a single great experience into a reliably positive learning design you and your students will continue to enjoy—and turn even a bad experience into something worthwhile.

Questions for Reflection

- How do you currently use technology to support differentiated instruction?
- Which technologies best support differentiation and administrative, operational, and pedagogical uses?
- How can technology goals and objectives for your students support differentiated instruction?
- How will you support students who join your class later in the academic year?

3

Creating a Community for Learning

This chapter covers...

- The characteristics of learning communities.
- What's special about learning communities in differentiated classrooms.
- How to foster a community that creates belonging and offers support for differentiated learning.
- How to use digital tools to make a learning community more equitable, efficient, effective, and engaging.

Whether learning occurs in person, online, or in a blended/hybrid format, the members of the learning community can contribute to (or work against) achieving the goals of differentiation. When everyone in the classroom recognizes, values, and supports one another, a group of students becomes more than a collection of individuals who share time and space as they strive toward individual achievement. They are an alliance—a community that is capable of learning with and from one another as they master standards and continue to grow in knowledge, understanding, and skills.

What Is a Learning Community?

Before designing a learning community (or *classroom community*) to support differentiated instruction, it's important to consider what one is and how it relates to learning. An appreciation of the benefits such communities offer in support of learning and learners helps teachers to envision the kind of environment they hope to create and to design the plans that will enlist their students' assistance in achieving it.

A **community** is a unified group of individuals who have common characteristics and come together around shared purposes and goals. There are as many different types of communities as there are groups of people coming together around common purposes and goals. In all cases, however, members willingly behave in ways that support the community, and the community, in turn, provides certain benefits to all members.

The behaviors required of members vary by community, but all community members intentionally forgo a degree of personal freedom to practice specific responsibilities that the community values. In exchange, the community is stronger and better able to offer its members different benefits, including security, stability, a sense of identity, and the social and emotional support that result from relating with others.

The members of a **learning community** come together around the shared purpose of learning and the goal of developing the skills, knowledge, and dispositions required for success in school and beyond. It includes the students, teachers, and others who support the goals and purposes of the class. Classes vary by level, subject area, the amount of time they spend together, the duration of their shared learning experience, and where and how their interactions occur (e.g., in person, online).

As with all communities, the strength of a learning community depends on how willing members are to support the whole—and on the whole's ability to provide benefits to its component members. A learning community is more likely to achieve its goals when students know what is expected of them (e.g., certain behaviors) and when they receive the support they need to be successful in performing them (e.g., focused instruction and practice, aid growing in self-awareness). Including students in identifying which behaviors are expected is critical. It promotes the students' understanding, acceptance, and practice of the behaviors that are important to the community's success. But a successful learning community must also offer something that the members need. This might include positive feelings of association (e.g., belonging, pride, joy), or it might fulfill other member needs (e.g., safety, support, nourishment). Successful learning communities acknowledge and plan for member needs. A community's ability to provide what members need to thrive rarely happens naturally; it is an intentional act that must be planned for or instigated.

The availability and power of communications technologies presents educators with expanded options for the kind of environments where learning communities can interact (e.g., a brick-and-mortar school, a virtual space, or some combination of the two) and *how* they interact (e.g., synchronous, asynchronous, blended/hybrid). These same technologies have also expanded who may be a part of a learning community. For example, videoconferencing makes it possible and easier to include ill or hospitalized students in the learning community. Their peers may still meet face-to-face, but such students can connect synchronously or asynchronously using digital tools. Likewise, learning management systems and other technologies make it possible to establish virtual classrooms even when there is disruption to physical class meetings, due to weather-, health-, or building-related concerns.

It is important to note that these new spaces for a classroom community don't just enable more numerous and different forms of interactions among community members—they can also increase the amount of time available for community engagement, extending the possibilities for connection beyond the length of the traditional school day. Students can continue to learn freely in groups online after school, on weekends, and over holiday breaks.

What Are the Characteristics of a Differentiated Learning Community?

Because a differentiated learning community is a type of learning community, **learning and success are shared goals and priorities**. However, in this particular type of learning community, there is a distinctive understanding of what "success" means. Mastering academic content knowledge is important, but students also expect, and also are expected, to learn about themselves and the dynamics of community participation.

In a differentiated learning community, **understanding oneself and what community participation involves are important** counterpoints to every learning experience—"melodies" played in conjunction with the curriculum content's main themes. Students engage in regular practice of self-assessment and reflection—not just to improve their academic performance but to gain self-knowledge. They come to recognize their gifts, talents, and challenges and learn how they learn best. Likewise, students informally study the advantages and demands of community participation. They find their work is enriched (e.g., made better or more rewarding) through exchanges (e.g., collaboration, peer assessment) and interactions (e.g., friendships, connections) with peers. They also learn about the demands and benefits of supporting and affirming others. Over time they learn to value their peers as unique, important individuals who each add something special to the group. These lessons set them up for positive experiences in the many communities they will encounter throughout their lives.

In a differentiated learning community, **educational "success" extends beyond mastery of academic standards**; it encompasses each student's development of the competencies required for continued learning. Every learner is expected to become proficient in skills that build their self-advocacy, agency, and independence (e.g., asking for help, self-monitoring, self-assessment). Students learn to value collaboration and the social skills this requires. In setting greater expectations for student success—rather than reducing them—participation in a differentiated learning community makes achievement more possible and probable (Mavidou & Kakana, 2019; Reis et al., 2011).

In a differentiated learning community, **relationships take on special significance**. Students experience them as sources of joy, inspiration, and educational support. This is why strategies such as peer tutoring, flexible grouping, and group processing are frequently used—strategically leveraged to promote both individual and collective success. Teachers, too, recognize the significance of such relationships and their practical instructional benefit. Through an ongoing dialogue, these relationships enable a regular flow of information that positively affects instruction. Teachers learn to appreciate the special character and identity of each student; an understanding of student needs and assets productively directs instructional decision making. Conversations with students, for example, might reveal common interests or common needs, informing future grouping decisions. Teachers can apply insights about students gained through conversation and observation over time to inform content choices and create more engaging and effective lessons, as we explain in Chapter 6.

Relationships knit the community tightly together. They also become a powerful means for enabling its continued, shared progress.

Designing a Differentiated Learning Community

Teachers who create a learning environment that supports differentiation benefit from a mindset that allows them to recognize the goals they are trying to achieve. What can you do to promote and affirm the development of personal behaviors that are conducive to learning? How can you create a structure for relationships and the kind of engagement that offers educational and social support for learning? How will your classroom embody the mission of differentiation—promoting optimal learning, achievement, and growth for all?

Consider the Goals

All differentiated learning communities **share the same goals** and must function in a way that achieves them. Those common goals are to

- Affirm the uniqueness of all members and the importance of their successful participation.
- Promote the acceptance and appreciation of students' diverse backgrounds, personalities, and experiences as learners.
- Enable the development of authentic and supportive relationships among community members.
- Stimulate the optimal development of both individual students and the community as a whole.
- Encourage the growth of dispositions and competencies that prepare each student to enjoy lifelong engagement in different relationships and communities.
- Promote and affirm the development of personal behaviors that are conducive to learning.
- Establish an environment that is socially and emotionally safe and, thus, conductive to risk taking and growth.

- Create a structure for relationships and engagement that offers educational, social, and other support for learning.
- Embody the mission of differentiation—promoting optimal learning, achievement, and growth for all.

Develop a Vision

A welcoming and supportive differentiated learning community is more likely to be achieved when its development is inspired by a clear vision. A *vision* is a mental image of what will be achieved from a collaborative, creative effort. In the simplest terms, it's the answer to the question "What type of community experience do teachers and students want to have together?" A vision illustrates what the community will be and how its members will interact, and it creatively expresses the shared understanding of what teachers and students commit to creating and sustaining together.

Because it describes a shared experience, formulating the vision for the community should also be communal and shared. It must represent and involve all members. Everyone in the community participates in naming what it will be like, how it will function, and how it will address everyone's needs and expectations. Formulating a shared vision increases the motivation community members will have to achieve it. What's more, the collaborative nature of crafting a vision and activities associated with designing it (e.g., brainstorming and discussions) gives students a chance to listen to, learn from, and begin appreciating one another. This work builds connections among community members and a sense of collective purpose. It also serves as an inspiration that motivates each constituent to invest in its attainment.

Although you and your students will develop the core vision for your differentiated classroom community, you can expand it with input from other community members—paraprofessionals or aides, volunteers, and others who spend time in your classroom (e.g., colleagues, instructional specialists). The vision should embody your professional aspirations for a differentiated practice and community, but you want it to evolve over time to incorporate input from its members and new information. For this reason, make your initial vision detailed but not rigid. The best visions allow for necessary reworking or additional iterations once the implementation of a plan reflects new details.

The more vivid and descriptive the vision of a learning community is, the better—and the easier it will be to articulate goals and develop plans and to achieve such a community. Consider the following questions when formulating a vision for your learning community:

- If a visitor were describing the learning community to someone else, what words—nouns, adjectives, and verbs—would they use?
- What would members of the learning community say about being a part of it? How do they feel about learning within it every day? What might they say about it on a Monday morning? In the middle of the week? On a Friday afternoon?
- What do members of the learning community give to it and receive from it? How is it equitable and engaging?
- How is this learning community connected to its educational purposes—especially those related to differentiation? How does it promote equitable, efficient, engaging, and effective learning for its members?
- How does technology—administrative, operational, and pedagogical—influence this learning community? Which technologies are important? Does the use of technology positively influence its members and what they do? How does using technology affect who is able to participate in this learning community? Is this consistent with the vision?
- What will members of the learning community learn about themselves and others, given what they do in the community and how it functions?
- What will "success" look like in the learning community? How will members know when it is functioning as they hope it will? How will this be acknowledged and celebrated?
- How is this learning community distinct and special when compared with other learning communities?

Design Plans to Achieve the Vision

Once you have established a vision for your differentiated learning community, the next step is to design plans that make achieving it possible. This involves translating the descriptive vision into concrete, actionable steps that are aligned with the goals of differentiation (see Figure 3.1).

FIGURE 3.1
Aligning Vision, Goals, and Plans for Actionable Steps

Vision	Goal	Actions
Everyone will feel that others are glad they are a part of the community and that they have an important contribution to make to the group.	In our learning community, each member will be treated as a valued member whose presence and participation in the community is important.	• We will create a code of conduct that sets the standard for welcoming, including, and valuing others, including actions to take when the code is and is not followed. • We will incorporate regular practices (e.g., at the end of group work, quarterly as part of the grading period) that allow us to affirm one another's contributions to learning and our community interactions.
Everyone will enjoy being a part of this special community; we recognize that, to grow, individuals might struggle from time to time.	We will strive to make our learning community a joyful and positive place and intentionally support one another in overcoming obstacles that get in the way.	We will begin each class with a verbal commitment (our class pledge) to remaining positive and supporting each other.

The teacher is primarily responsible for designing a plan that reflects the vision of the group and may want to use operational technologies to assist in doing so. A design board—sometimes called a *mood board* by interior designers—is a space that assists creative designers with visualizing their ideas. Design boards make it easier to keep track of ideas related to the vision, consider the synthesis of different ideas, and creatively generate new ones. Each object on the board—text, graphics, photos, and color swatches—represents an idea. Shared virtual workspaces (e.g., IdeaBoardz, Padlet, Wakelet) and social media networks that feature image sharing (e.g., Pinterest) can help teachers envision how the physical aspects of the environment might contribute to the community described in the vision. Design boards can help represent ideas that address the physical (e.g., classroom layout, lighting, colors) and non-physical (e.g., support for interpersonal interactions) aspects of the environment. Project management tools (e.g., Basecamp, monday, Zoho) can help track steps to achieving the vision, share timelines, and support community sharing of materials.

Individual differentiation goals dictate who participates in developing the plans to meet them. Depending on the details of the context (e.g., age of students, amount of time available), teachers can decide how much to involve others in designing plans. As a rule of thumb, a plan to achieve the vision goals is more likely to be successful when students have some degree of involvement. At the very least, students should be able to see and react to plans that have been designed.

Evaluate the Design

It helps to evaluate progress as the plans for developing the learning community are implemented and at various points across the academic year. Considering how the community is functioning and if it is meeting the goals established for it allows for further refinement and growth. Evaluation also helps identify plans that need adjusting or additional actionable steps that need to be taken. Consider the following questions when appraising and adjusting plans:

- Are the stated goals in the plan consistent with those for a differentiated learning community? Which are most supportive? Which should be adjusted?
- Which of the set goals are being met? Which plans associated with them are working? What parts of the plan need adjustment? What are we learning?

- Which goals must we still strive to achieve? What barriers or challenges do we face? What can be done to address them? What are we learning?
- What aspects of the plan might need to be adapted to ensure stronger support for differentiation? How could the plan be made more equitable?
- How is the integration of operational, administrative, and pedagogical technology influencing and supporting what goes on in this learning community? How could the mix be adjusted to offer stronger support for the community? Should we use more, less, or different technology?
- Are there additional supports or resources that could strengthen the community? How can we secure them?

Expand and Extend the Community with Technology

The increased availability and broader acceptance of communication technologies make it possible for educators to reconsider who can be a part of a learning community—and how to extend it. Today's education settings do not require physical presence in "real time" or limit who can participate. Family members, subject-matter experts, and local community members might contribute to and support the learning community's goals and purposes. For example, grandparents who do not live close to the school could provide support for students' reading practice. Family members who travel for work or live far away can attend and give feedback on virtual student learning showcases. Subject-matter experts can participate in classroom discussions through videoconferencing or support students' research projects via asynchronous conferencing. Think of what the potential benefits of this additional adult supervision from volunteers might be in terms of students' ability to interact with content experts and mentors.

An expanded idea of what constitutes a learning community has great promise for the differentiated classroom. The virtual dimension can be leveraged to make the learning community bigger, enabling more people to benefit from the beauty and joy of being part of such a community. It could also make the learning community better, providing greater support for individual and communal learning. Of course, new possibilities for community members do not change the need to adhere to existing school policies and practices that protect students and maintain their privacy. Any plans for expanding the community will benefit from administrative approval and processes that weigh benefits and eliminate risks. For example, it is best to get permission from the school administration before inviting anyone to speak or present—in person or virtually—to your students.

Technology also can change when, how, and how much students in the learning community connect with one another. Extending connections outside the classroom setting can increase support for learning and other interactions. Would it benefit your community to have more time for group work, to provide flexibility for students who are more comfortable working outside the school environment, or to have animations or recorded classroom presentations for later reviewing to support student understandings?

Key Practices for Differentiated Learning Communities

It takes both planning and action to create a learning community with the mindset and skill set to support effective differentiation. There are various ways that educational designers might pursue this, and the approach will vary from one differentiated learning community to the next. Among these approaches, we've identified some powerful practices that can assist teachers in achieving their plans: (1) developing a shared identity, (2) building relationships and connections, and (3) using games to get students excited about bonding.

Develop a Shared Identity

One of the most important tasks in creating a community that optimally supports each individual student involves cultivating a shared social identity—a mechanism through which students establish links and connections with one another and come to think of their class as "us."

Developing a shared identity among class members helps students focus on their collective learning needs. It's a way for the diverse and unique individuals in a classroom to acknowledge their common destiny and embrace the plans that support individual success. Teachers who successfully cultivate a shared identity will have students who draw close personal associations to the community as a whole and who feel a sense of connection, loyalty, and commitment to their classmates. This sense of group identity is a solid foundation for effective differentiation. Students are better able to cooperate and collaborate. They feel like they belong and develop the trust that makes giving feedback, receiving it, and learning together easier. Further, where a group identity is experienced, there are positive effects for individual students with regard to self-esteem, self-efficacy, assertiveness, and empathy, as well as satisfaction with life and academic performance (Paricio et al., 2020). Students who accept their mutual connections are more likely to accept responsibility for behaving and acting in ways that support the community and one other.

Teachers need to identify the various elements of the shared identity of a class before it can be cultivated and connected with by the students. The available time, level of learners, subject area, and personality of community members are all important to consider. The identity will reflect the vision and goals included in the community design, but it should also capture the shared characteristics of the students, as well as the purposes and specific mission for their learning in a particular subject, school, or grade.

As with the vision, goals, and plans, the learning community's identity should represent all its members. Even though the teacher has ultimate creative control in the process, student input is essential. During the process, listen to student opinions—gathered through whole-class discussion, responses to an online survey, or informal conversations with individual students and groups of students. Elements of a differentiated learning community's identity include the following:

- **A mission statement** that defines what the community is and why it is special. Developing a mission statement builds awareness of the community's shared characteristics, purpose, and goals.
- **A community slogan or motto** that captures the essence of the community and allows its identity to be communicated simply and consistently.
- **A physical representation of the community identity.** This promotes recognition and acceptance of the community, and makes it easier to identify, understand, and remember. It can be anything from a simple graphic or image to a song or jingle, a hashtag, a video

or cartoon, or some kind of collectable (e.g., figurines, pens, tote bags).

Teachers take different approaches when developing a classroom identity. Some find it valuable to work with the class or class representatives to collect input. Others begin by involving the class in developing a mission statement and then hold contests to select the class logo, slogan, and so on. Regardless of how the learning community is developed, it should capture the guiding principles of differentiation and be inclusive of all class members as much as possible. Figure 3.2 presents an example of a worksheet a teacher might use to capture community identity.

Build Relationships and Connections

The loyalty, unity, and bonds the students develop when they connect with a classroom's identity are vital for creating a differentiated learning community. Teachers need to purposefully cultivate support for relationships rather than leaving this to chance. Let's examine a few strategies that are helpful.

Highlight individual students. "Student spotlights" are a relationship-cultivating strategy that works well across grade levels and subject areas. In student spotlights, attention is focused on learning about each student's unique attributes (e.g., family members, birthdate, favorite foods, colors, travel locations). This activity allows students to get to know things about one another that might not otherwise surface in the interactions they have while learning academic content and encourages them to appreciate the unique characteristics of their peers and find those with similar or intersecting traits. These points of comparison and contrast can give rise to conversations and, eventually, to bonds and relationships. In the early grades, this activity is often built into the school day as a way of meeting language arts learning standards.

Students vary in how comfortable they are sharing personal information and details, so proceed with caution and empathy. First, give students an option about which information is shared. For example, students who do not live with their parents could feel uncomfortable sharing information about their family; students who do not regularly go on vacation may feel embarrassed indicating this on a spotlight template. Presenting students

FIGURE 3.2
Learning Community Identity Worksheet

Mission Statement	Room 4C, also known as *Mrs. B's Brilliant Bookworms,* is a collaborative community of distinct learners who bring their best to promote optimal growth and learning about content and one another. It strives to be the best class in the whole state of Arkansas.
Logo	Five bookworms in the school colors, intertwined to form a heart shape with a star in the middle.
Song	"Best Day of My Life," American Authors, determined by student vote.
Motto/Slogan	• "We learn the best when we care the most!" • "Here we work together to achieve our individual best!" • Combined from several proposed by student teams.
Ways to Communicate and Reinforce Our Community Identify	• Include logo on newsletters, classroom blog page, other official materials. Slogan at the bottom of email signature and displayed on classroom door. Plan for a special T-shirt and pencils. • Test students on the meaning of the objects in the logo and what they symbolize. Students memorize and explain the mission statement. Students create slogans to add to room décor in a contest with the first prize being lunch with the teacher! • Classroom management plan tied into logo. Tables compete to create the completed classroom logo; they get one design element put on the classroom chart each time they attain a behavioral goal. Rewards are available upon completion.

with a long list from which they can select points to share is more responsive to student differences. Such a list often includes "favorites" (e.g., food, place, song, movie, color, season, activities, pet) or basic biographical information (e.g., important people in the student's life) but could also include

- Languages spoken;
- Activity the student would undertake if time and money were no issue;

- Something everyone should know about them;
- Famous person, living or dead, the student most wants to meet and why;
- What they would change if they were in charge of the school; and
- A new holiday they would add to the national calendar.

Discover differences. As students get to know one another and find common connections, they become more able and receptive to learning about one another's differences. Survey tools are an excellent way to focus on important and interesting differences as they relate to general topics, learning preferences, content-area learning, and the classroom. Depending on the classroom context, you may want to steer students toward finding differences that will enhance your differentiated practice. For example, you could explore differences that have relevance to the creation of functional groups. If you plan for students to work in groups as they develop a digital poster as a final assessment, you will want to inventory students' different talents—who can create a graphic? Organize and keep the team on task? Log progress and maintain a schedule for completion? Interpret the rubric and explain it to others? Such information results in the construction of more functional groups, while also giving you insights into students' strengths and abilities you can highlight with the class.

Secure survey tools (e.g., Google Forms, SurveyMonkey) make it easy to create a digital survey and share it with students. Students respond to the survey individually and then go back and explore the results from their peers. Open-ended items are easy to write but can be difficult to analyze. Close-ended objective items (e.g., multiple choice, true/false, checkboxes) are harder to write but easier to analyze; results appear in a table or chart.

Use Games to Promote Bonding

Engaging students in bonding activities allows them to get to know you, the teacher, as well as one another. It helps build trust, loyalty, and unity; experiencing these feelings, in turn, can have a positive effect on student behavior (Beaty-O'Ferrall et al., 2010). The cooperation required is a reminder that what they do and say to others matters. When students are on task and manage their behavior, it supports the learning others do and contributes to the success of the class as a whole. Individual and group relationships build additional layers of cohesion.

Designing plans that employ strategies for cultivating relationships takes time and purposeful planning—one such strategy, using games, can build student trust and camaraderie in an engaging way. Contests that highlight the way that students are unique (e.g., most freckles, most unusual pet, most easy-going) can be a great way to recognize individuals—provided that all students are recognized in ways that are positive and appropriate. These activities have the effect of making students feel "seen" and "known." Team-building games (e.g., the human knot, blanket switch, obstacle course, scavenger hunt), appropriate to the age-level and interests of the class, can also be helpful.

Using Digital Tools to Address the 4Es and Respond to Barriers

As noted in Chapter 2, when considering educational technology use, the selection criteria should include a digital tool's ability to further equitable, efficient, engaging, and effective instruction. Sometimes the ways in which a digital tool will support these ends are clear and the effects of its use will be immediate and easy to document; other times, a tool's benefits are less obvious, and its use is an investment in and a foundation for future gains. Let's look now at a few of the ways that digital tool use can support the work of community building, which helps to create the conditions for greater equity, efficiency, engagement, and efficiency and for widespread student success.

Digital Flash Cards

As mentioned previously, games that help students recognize one another's faces and learn important details about their classmates often have a lot of appeal and are generally useful in developing relationships. However, not all students find games an effective way of getting to know their peers, and most games do not include multimedia supports that promote equitable expression of important information.

Digital flash cards (e.g., Brainscape, Cram, Quizlet) have several affordances. They offer multiple modes for sharing information (e.g., images, text, sound) that innately help students learn about one another. Students who have difficulty recognizing their classmates' appearance (e.g., some students with autism spectrum disorder) benefit from electronic flash cards that incorporate photo snapshots of their peers and can practice as much as needed. Everyone receives additional support in learning to pronounce less common or difficult-to-pronounce names. Digital flash cards can also be accessed by more than one person at a time and reviewed anywhere using digital devices, including outside the classroom (i.e., student use of the flash cards does not have to interfere with academic learning time).

There are a couple of constraints with digital flash cards. If students are going to share personal information online, you will need to ensure their safety. Student information should never be shared in an insecure or non-password-protected space. As with choosing other digital tools, you will need to ensure that using digital flash cards meets the acceptable-use guidelines of your school or district. To help students learn to exercise good sense when sharing personal data with their classmates, you may need to provide some guidelines for what is and is not appropriate and review these flash cards before they are accessible to the community.

Polling

The faster students start finding connections with one another, the sooner they can tap into the benefits gained from relating to one another and sharing a social identity. Increased self-esteem, enjoyment, and learning unique lessons about classmates are some of the powerful and positive by-products of relationships, beginning when individuals first connect over what they have in common and progress as they explore their differences. Although students vary in how long it takes to relate to others, the process usually involves some time.

Although there are some constraints to consider (e.g., polling tends to identify superficial connections that may not create real bonds among students unless there are opportunities to go deeper), online polling tools (e.g., Poll Everywhere, Socrative) offer numerous affordances. They can increase engagement, raise interest, and aid in making connections. Students respond to teacher-created polls on a device (e.g., phone, web browser), making it easy for teachers to poll students as they reply to different questions and then share the combined responses with the class. Questions to ask will depend on when the polls are used and other aspects of the classroom context (e.g., age of students, subject area). Many teachers involve students in developing the questions, which not only encourages students to take ownership but also ensures that students feel comfortable answering the questions. Plus, students often create excellent ideas and appreciate opportunities to contribute.

Strive to develop polling prompts to identify points of commonality instead of differences. It can work well to craft prompts so they can be answered with "yes" or "no" (see Figure 3.3). Follow-up discussion could include questions to identify which students responded in the same way.

The type of connections found through polling may seem simplistic, but the idea is for students to begin recognizing that they have a lot in common with one another and different things in common with different classmates. Building this sense of familiarity introduces them to other students outside their "friend group."

You can plan polling like this by building it into your daily agenda—asking several questions at the beginning or end of every class session or at the beginning and end of learning units. In this way, the practice becomes a regular feature of the classroom, students gradually learn more about one another, and you have an intriguing attention-getting activity. Share one to two prompts at a time, and then give students a few moments to find someone they do not know well who responded in the same way and talk for a few minutes about their responses to promote bonding before addressing academic content. If students cannot find someone who responded in the same way, they locate a peer who also gave a unique answer and connect with them.

Virtual or Remote Participants

It can be difficult for one teacher to single-handedly support the success of a differentiated learning community, including both the creation of this community and the learning that goes on within it. Technology can make it possible to include additional people in an extended learning community—those who can offer assistance, encouragement, and accountability for learning as well as contribute to the cohesion and feeling of the community. Many teachers rely on in-person volunteers, people who have been screened (e.g., often with background checks) and approved to engage with the students as instructional aides or mentors. They are used to inviting family members to be part of the classroom "audience" at certain culminating student presentations. Increasingly, however, teachers are finding it helpful to augment their communities with virtual or remote participants. Again, these community members must be similarly approved of and monitored to ensure student safety, security, and comfort.

FIGURE 3.3
Sample Polling Questions

General Likes and Dislikes	I like the food in the school cafeteria. I like days off school. I think summer is the best season. My birthday is my favorite holiday. I think the best breakfast is pancakes. I think dogs are better pets than cats. I like to read. I like to sleep in late. I like pizza. I like hot weather.
Learning Preferences	I prefer learning by seeing something. I prefer learning by doing something physical. I prefer learning by hearing something.
Content-Area Learning	I like fantasy literature. I like poetry. I like reading or watching the news. I think writing a letter is enjoyable. I would like to have lived in ancient Egypt. I think chemistry is interesting.
Classroom Environment	I think the class seating arrangement is a good one. I think the resources we have access to in this classroom are well-organized. I think our teacher gives us enough time to get our work done. I think our classroom seating is comfortable.

In the early grades, grandparents or other relatives might be invited to connect with the whole class via videoconferencing (e.g., Zoom, Microsoft Teams), serving as part of the audience for class presentations or acting as reading buddies who provide individual monitoring, intervention, and cheerleading for individuals and small groups of students. In the higher grades, family members and others (e.g., preservice teachers, community volunteers) might be involved in celebrations of learning using social media tools (e.g., VoiceThread, Padlet), providing formative comments on projects as they develop, contributing their voices and experience to enrich discussion, or adding color and joy (e.g., sharing a thought for the day or an inspirational quote related to the community theme).

Exploring different ways for the learning community to include parents, family members, and others makes for more equitable participation and is an important affordance of this strategy. Online chat, discussion groups, and videoconferencing can make it possible for those who have difficulty being physically present (e.g., those who are home-bound, live out of state, do not have transportation or sufficient time to get to the school) to participate, increasing equity. Online access supports community members dropping in on an individual basis and invites participation from those whose work schedules are more rigid (e.g., those in customer service or healthcare). Additional possibilities for including a diverse group in the extended learning community might include the use of translation tools for multilingual learners and audio captioning, which is now available with most videoconference platforms (e.g., Zoom, Teams). One constraint is that not all people will have access to the technology or the skills required to use it.

Communication Tools

Communication is connection. Without communication, there is no connection between individuals. In a differentiated learning community, effective communication—whether between students and their teacher, among students, or between the teacher and members of the extended learning community—is of paramount importance. Effective communication is how important information is shared, relationships deepen, and various types of learning (e.g., intellectual, social, emotional) are supported.

Many different types of digital tools can support effective communication about student performance, behavior, assignments, and events. Each offers affordances and constraints that must be carefully weighed to consider how they affect the equitable participation of all learning community members. Be aware of different tools' potential benefits, but do not assume their use will have a positive influence. It's essential to periodically check in to ascertain the degree to which each tool is being used to its fullest by different students and community members.

Administrative technologies (e.g., PowerSchool) facilitate communicating important information about students, including their performance data in real time (e.g., as soon as a teacher enters a record of student progress). If parents and caregivers know how to monitor student progress, they can intervene quickly to support students when needed. However, it is not always the case that monitoring is occurring in a student's home; you will need to determine to what extent you can rely on this feature to keep families informed and involved. Perhaps most families can benefit, but you may also need to reach out through a phone call or email.

With **learning management systems** (e.g., Blackboard, Canvas, Google Classroom), you can provide students and their families with up-to-date information about assignments and materials for completion in an organized, user-friendly, virtual space. However, some students may have difficulty navigating the interface or understanding the information (e.g., if they struggle to read or are multilingual learners).

Class social media sites (e.g., Facebook, Instagram), web pages (e.g., Google Sites, Squarespace, Weebly, Wix, WordPress), and other **classroom communication tools** (e.g., ClassDojo, Seesaw) make it easy to share newsletters, updates, events, and photos. They can also, in some instances, connect members of the extended learning community to one another via concealed email addresses. Text-based tools (e.g., GroupMe, Remind101) are another convenient way to share short, timely, secure messages that can be archived. Still, bear in mind your goal of equitable participation in the community for all classroom members: do not assume that all have the technologies, electronic access, time, language proficiency, and technical skills to participate equally.

The Communication Plan

Digital tools can help you, as an educational designer, build a learning community that supports all students to the fullest. However, for each tool to work optimally, you need to have a strategic plan for implementation—and this plan should be shared with the learning community so that everyone knows when, how, and why they will be used.

If you are invested in all members participating in communication equitably, you will also want to consider what support they might need—instructions for downloading a special app? Access to tutorials? Netiquette guidelines? It is important to note that it need not be the teacher's sole responsibility to provide this support; in some cases, all it takes is sharing links or asking for volunteers to help other community members. As the leader of the community, you will want to be sensitive to promoting welcome and offering guidance.

At the beginning of the school year, draw up your communication plan (see Figure 3.4). It should include

1. The communication channels that will be used,
2. What types of information will be shared, and
3. The methods of use (i.e., time for release and frequency).

Also let community members know when they can expect responses from email, phone, or text messages (e.g., within 48 hours during the typical work week) and your preferred methods for communications. Finally, ensure that the plan is understood by all community members (i.e., get all to "sign off" on it).

FIGURE 3.4
Sample Communication Plan

Communication Channel	Type of Information Shared	Frequency	Monitoring
Hard-copy materials	School announcements (*Note:* This classroom will strive for being a paperless communications environment.)	Because it is difficult to predict when the school will require hard-copy materials sent home, a Remind101 text will be sent to families as an alert.	• Students are responsible for ensuring the material arrives home. • Parents are responsible for reading it and reaching out with questions to the teacher or school office.
Canvas learning management system	• Assignments • Materials for assignments • Assignment calendar	Ongoing/daily basis with a weekly update	• Students are responsible for checking regularly. It is possible to set up text/email "push" notifications about updates. • Parents can "opt in" to checking.
PowerSchool	• Grades (recorded as they are generated) • Mass emails to families/caregivers • Individual emails to families/students	Sporadic	• Parents and students are responsible for checking regularly. • It is possible to set up text/email "push" notifications about updates.

(*continued*)

FIGURE 3.4—(*continued*)
Sample Communication Plan

Communication Channel	Type of Information Shared	Frequency	Monitoring
Email reminders	Mass emails with urgent or important information that did not get sent through other channels.	Sporadic	Parents are primarily responsible.
Instagram	Photos (provided students give permission to post)	Sporadic	This is open to the larger learning community to monitor through their apps which give "push" notifications.

Questions for Reflection

- What administrative, operational, and pedagogical technologies are available to you and your students? How can these be used to support creating a classroom learning community?
- How well do available technologies meet 4E criteria? Can you make better use of these technologies with the 4Es in mind as you consider the classroom learning community? What areas do you wish to focus on?
- Are there learning community needs that existing technologies are not adequately addressing? What additional or improved technologies would help you gain a better understanding of your students and their parents?
- What are your goals and objectives for integrating technology to support the classroom learning community? How will you incorporate these goals and objectives during the academic year?

4

Designing and Using Pre-assessment

This chapter covers...

- The role of pre-assessment in differentiation.
- How to set goals for and plan for pre-assessment.
- The key practices that promote effective pre-assessment.
- How to use digital tools to reduce barriers and address the 4Es during pre-assessment.

Appreciating students as people—grasping their stories, struggles, and dreams for the future—creates a bond that supports successful learning. Teachers skilled at differentiating instruction recognize that understanding their students as learners is necessary to design instruction that aligns with students' needs and strengths. Over time and with practice, these teachers become increasingly adept at initiating meaningful conversations, asking powerful questions, being careful listeners, and using digital tools to learn what their students require to succeed. They develop this skill set through the regular use of pre-assessment.

What Is Pre-assessment?

Pre-assessment is the focused inquiry teachers perform to learn about their students' current skill, knowledge, and mindset status before developing a unit, lesson, or learning sequence. Pre-assessment data informs instructional planning, ensuring that a teacher's decisions are grounded in actual information about students rather than assumptions about them. In other words, gathering and analyzing pre-assessment data is what allows you to teach the students you *have* rather than the students you *had last year*, the students you *think* you have, or the students you *wish* you had.

The information gained through pre-assessment has bearing on a variety of decisions that are foundational for effective differentiation, including the following:

- What else—what prerequisite knowledge or skills, for example—needs to be taught to help students meet the lesson or unit's learning objectives?
- Which instructional approaches will be most appropriate to use?
- How much time will the lesson or unit require?
- What types of grouping will be most appropriate?
- Which tools, resources, or materials will facilitate the successful completion of the learning activities?
- How can instruction be differentiated to address learner needs and instructional goals?

Teachers who gather, analyze, and use information from pre-assessment can design lessons that better challenge, motivate, and scaffold student learning. Additionally, involving students in the pre-assessment process provides them with information they can use to gain a better understanding of what they know (and do not know) in relation to the content they will be learning.

Although many aspects of pre-assessment are particular to the context in which it is being implemented, teachers often focus on gathering information about (1) students' foundational knowledge and skills and (2) students' experience in relation to the upcoming learning experience's target knowledge, understandings, and skills—sometimes referred to by Tomlinson (2017b) and others as "KUDs"—what students are expected to *k*now, *u*nderstand, and be able to *do* when instruction is complete.

Foundational Knowledge and Skills

Foundational knowledge and skills are the prerequisite capacities students need to successfully build *new* knowledge and skills. They are the ideas, concepts, and vocabulary that are instrumental to anticipated learning, as well as the abilities that contribute to it. If students lack the proper foundation, they struggle during the learning process and find it difficult to meet learning expectations. For example, a student who does not know the term *variable* will be confused when listening to instructions for how to solve an algebraic expression. A student who is unable to dribble a basketball will have difficulty learning to do a layup. Identifying which students have the requisite foundational knowledge and skills for an upcoming learning experience allows teachers to plan for interventions (e.g., re-teaching, grouping, providing a glossary) and to proceed in the most powerful way to promote individual and group success.

Mastery of the Targeted KUDs

The second category of information teachers aim to acquire through pre-assessment is students' experience with the knowledge, understandings, and skills (KUDs) that will be the focus of the lesson, learning sequence, or unit. Information about whether some students have already been exposed to or have already mastered aspects of the targeted content allows teachers to plan for learning experiences (e.g., tiered instruction, learning centers, choice menus) that offer each student an opportunity to grow while simultaneously promoting the success of the entire class. You can compare pre-assessment data to data captured in a summative assessment (see Chapter 5) at the end of a sequence or unit; this provides insight into how much students learned as well as how well they performed. Baseline mastery data gathered prior to instruction can also help you recognize your own instructional impact. Comparing pre-assessment data with summative assessment data can show you how your instructional decisions affect student learning.

The most effective pre-assessment does more than identify which students have already been exposed to upcoming content; it also helps to identify where students' mastery is lacking, generates information about which misconceptions and misunderstandings exist, and highlights common patterns or trends among students. All of this information can be applied to improve lesson design—and make it more targeted, relevant, and interesting. Misconceptions students reveal in their pre-assessments can highlight specific areas that could be a springboard into new learning. Teachers can also revise a lesson to address the misconception directly by adding a hands-on activity drawing ellipses to a unit on the solar system, for example, to address the misconception that planets move in a circular orbit around the sun.

Direct and Indirect Pre-assessment

Pre-assessment can be direct or indirect (Tomlinson & Moon, 2013). A **direct pre-assessment** is usually a required, formal measure (although it should always be a low-stakes, low-key measure) that typically occurs during part of the instructional day or for homework. Direct pre-assessments include such things as a survey consisting of Likert-type questions that students answer regarding goals, objectives, and content standards for the topic they will be learning. By contrast, an **indirect pre-assessment** is always informal and frequently involves a broad sweep of the class and very little instructional time. For instance, you might ask your class to give a (physical) thumbs up or down sign in response to a pre-assessment question; some teachers use digital clickers (i.e., student response tools) or online questionnaires. Using both direct and indirect pre-assessment provides you (and your students) with important information about what students know and need to know, and what misconceptions they might have.

Strategies for Pre-assessment

Let's look at three strategies commonly used for pre-assessment.

Open-ended surveys are a popular method. Many teachers use them to determine whether students possess mastery of the content that will be presented. For example, if you're introducing a unit in social studies and want to find out if and in what ways students understand the social studies concept of a *need,* you might ask them to complete the sentence, "When we talk about a *need* in social studies, it refers to ______." The specific understandings you uncover when looking at or listening to students' responses can be used to enrich the lesson and generate interest in the lesson.

Graphic organizers (e.g., KWL charts) are also commonly used; these tools inventory what students already know and what they want to know on the topic to be studied. Such tools have additional functions during and after learning takes place. If students use graphic organizers to record new ideas and understandings they gain across the learning process, the organizers can serve as "learning journals" that can be shared with others, such as family members, and as a record of learning that students can revisit.

End-of-unit tests can also be used for pre-assessment. When administered before learning takes place, they produce baseline data about existing exposure to targeted KUDs that you can compare to summative assessments (see Chapter 5), helping you gauge the extent of students' learning.

Pre-assessment in Differentiated Classrooms

Pre-assessment is beneficial in every educational setting, but it is an essential tool in differentiated ones. When differentiating instruction, what you know about your students influences every aspect of the learning process you design. The frequency with which you implement pre-assessment, the specific strategies you use to pre-assess, and how you apply the resulting data matters, and it must be intentional. When differentiation is a primary goal, the teacher's philosophical approach, the categories of information sought, and how students are involved all influence pre-assessment. You'll not only learn which knowledge and skills students already possess and which they need to develop, but you will also use pre-assessment data to design learning experiences that address students' readiness, interests, and learning profiles. In the differentiated classroom, teachers work to include students in the process, meaning that they too are asked to focus on understanding what they know, what they need to learn, and what misconceptions they might have.

One distinctive characteristic of pre-assessment in a differentiated classroom has to do with the scope of information that teachers aim to discover. Information on students' foundational knowledge and existing mastery related to targeted content is part of determining student readiness. To this information, you add information about students' interests and learning profile and use these three factors in combination to inform your learning design and all the decisions you make to differentiate the content, process, products, and environments associated with instruction (see Figure 4.1).

Here's another distinguishing characteristic of pre-assessment in a differentiated classroom: teachers recognize that the method of student inquiry influences the data acquired on students' readiness, interest, and learning profile. Various methods of inquiry—from interviews to the incorporation of technology—may be appropriate, depending on learner characteristics (e.g., age, comfort with different modes of inquiry). For example, you might ask students to create a video recording of their problem-solving process in math (i.e., an operational digital tool) and then review it to understand how prepared students are for a new lesson. This approach could enable a richer understanding of students' strengths, areas of weakness, and interest. Or you might consider administrative technologies such as a digital portfolio or file storage system to keep track of student information from pre-assessment, including who has completed it and who has not (e.g., due to absences). Information collected in this manner would make comparing the learning performance easier across stages of learning.

FIGURE 4.1
Information Collected Through Pre-assessment

DI Element	Type of Information Collected
Readiness	• Foundational knowledge and skills to be built on during the upcoming learning sequence • Existing mastery of the knowledge and skills to be addressed in the upcoming learning sequence • Misunderstandings or misconceptions that may affect upcoming student learning
Learning profile	• How a student's gender, culture, well-being, and learning preferences will influence an upcoming learning sequence
Interest	• Degree of interest in the topics and activities involved in the upcoming learning sequence • Interests that might support success in the upcoming learning sequence • Common interests among students

Designing and Using Pre-assessment

Powerful use of pre-assessment—productively identifying aspects that positively affect student learning—is possible when teachers approach it with the mindset of a designer. Developing a broad plan for the school year as well as plans for specific assessments (e.g., for a particular lesson or unit) repays the investment of time and energy. Teachers, as well as students, benefit from a philosophical approach to pre-assessment and understanding all the ways practicing it influences their efforts to differentiate. Goal-setting can help you identify what you hope to accomplish and clarify the benefits you anticipate from pre-assessment. Explaining the purpose of pre-assessment and engaging students in the process is also critical in meeting other differentiation goals (e.g., helping them become independent learners).

Focus on a Holistic Understanding of Students

Among the many factors influencing instructional decision making (e.g., available time, required resources, teacher preferences), the most important one is the attributes of the students themselves. This is why it's crucial to devote considerable time and energy to learning about your students. Your appreciation for and approach to relationships are at the heart of designing instruction that is truly responsive—and your use of pre-assessment will reflect this.

Because each student is a complete and unique person, a key aim for pre-assessment is to gain a more holistic understanding of who each student is. In addition to seeking to understand where students struggle, you also want to better understand each one's personal disposition, cultural background, talents, and gifts. For example, if you're preparing to teach 1st graders about the concept of time and how to "tell time," you will want to know whether students understand important terminology (e.g., *minute hand, hour, clock*) and can already perform the procedural steps involved in telling time (e.g., complete a checklist of instructions). Do students understand the benefit of telling time (e.g., they can explain it helps a person arrive punctually at various events)? Have they had exposure to different types of clocks (e.g., with Roman numerals, analog, digital)? Do they understand different expressions related to telling time (e.g., "lunch time," "class time")? With a well-rounded sense of students and their assets, teachers can tailor instructional supports and opportunities that will enrich the overall learning experience.

Demonstrating appreciation of students affirms their uniqueness and optimizes their success. This philosophy not only guides all forms of assessment (e.g., pre-assessment, formative assessment, summative assessment, self-assessment, peer assessment) but it also influences every aspect of the instructional process.

Set Goals for Pre-assessment

Your goals for using pre-assessments should relate to your philosophy and approach to assessment. Pre-assessments and plans for them should be designed in a way that will

- Clearly determine students' knowledge, skills, dispositions, attitudes, and interests vis-à-vis the targeted goals and objectives;
- Strategically identify details about students that will be most useful when designing and delivering instruction;
- Involve students as collaborators by sharing the purpose of the pre-assessment and explaining how the data will be used;
- Promote students' learning about themselves through self-analysis and reflection;
- Use time efficiently by generating data that allows for more efficient and effective instruction;
- Incorporate technology to support efficient recording, distribution, and analysis as well as effective application of the data acquired; and
- Integrate teachers' skills with assessment and decision making and their use of digital tools.

You'll need to consider how often you are going to use pre-assessment over the course of the year, semester, or quarter; what methods will work best; and how it might be used in a way that most benefits you and your students. You will also need to set goals for specific pre-assessments, which ensures that each is better able to fulfill its purpose. Figure 4.2 presents some questions to consider when setting your goals for general pre-assessments and specific pre-assessments.

FIGURE 4.2

Setting Goals for Pre-assessments: Questions to Consider

General Goals	Specific Unit or Lesson Goals
• How often will I use pre-assessments for instructional planning? • What direct and indirect pre-assessment measures are appropriate? • What are my priorities for inquiring about students through pre-assessments? What would be most powerful to know about my students? Why? • What tools and technologies will I use to distribute, analyze, and apply pre-assessment data? How will I ensure tools and tech are appropriate for my students and convey the best data possible? • How will students benefit from what I learn and what *they* learn through the pre-assessment process? How will I engage them in the process and in comprehending its purpose and their responsibilities? • How will I use pre-assessment data for planning lessons and units? Will what I learn allow me to curate better resources, materials, and tools to support their learning? • What changes might I need to make based on what I learn about student readiness, interest, and learning profiles? How will I modify the content, process, products, and environments associated with instruction? • As the year progresses, how will I refine my inquiry through pre-assessment? • How will what I learn from this year's students refine my expertise as a professional moving forward?	• What do I hope to learn from this pre-assessment? • What should I pre-assess? Is it more important to focus on students' readiness, interest, or learning profile? Some combination? Why? • How will I engage students in the pre-assessment process? • How can I promote my students' learning about themselves from this pre-assessment? Will I ask them to reflect on it after I have looked at the data? Would it be helpful to include in a portfolio that records information about their learning needs and interests? • What modifications might I make with the information I gain from the students? • What method will I use for this pre-assessment? If I select a digital tool, will it help make learning more equitable, efficient, effective, engaging? Are there drawbacks to using this tool?

Key Practices for Effective Pre-assessment

For pre-assessment to be optimally useful and generate the information teachers need to differentiate, it must be integrated strategically and regularly. This means incorporating pre-assessment in an intentional way and using the information gleaned from it to purposefully adapt instruction. Key practices include (1) prioritizing information to address through pre-assessment, (2) stimulating student learning, and (3) supporting students' needs.

Prioritize Information to Address

When planning pre-assessment in a differentiated classroom, it is important to consider the following:

- What, exactly, the pre-assessment should address (e.g., the specific knowledge, understandings, skills, and dispositions or information about areas of student variance);
- The type of pre-assessment it will be (direct or indirect);
- The information it will seek (e.g., to discover areas where the most students need support, the particular interests students have that might be built into the lesson);
- What will be involved in the implementation of the pre-assessment? How will it be distributed, collected, analyzed, and used?
- How useful is the information generated likely to be? What will it be used for, and how might the design for learning and experiences of learners be adjusted, depending on what the data reveal?

Some teachers find it helpful to use simple graphic tables, matrices, or Venn diagrams to identify and prioritize the information they are seeking (see Figure 4.3).

Stimulate Student Engagement

Decades of research consistently support the positive correlation between student engagement and student learning (see, for example, Cobb, 1972; Finn et al., 1995, 1997; Lahaderne, 1968; Samuels & Turnure, 1974). Valuable and engaging pre-assessment techniques help students connect cognitively with the content, recognize the value and purpose of

FIGURE 4.3
Pre-assessment Planning Matrix: Telling Time

Standard: Students will be able to tell time to the hour and half hour on digital and analog clocks.

Questions to Ask		Ways to Get Answers
Interest	• Is the child interested in telling time? • Are there ways that telling time might be important to the student?	At back-to-school night or using a parent survey, ask questions such as these: • Does your child have a concept of time? • Has your child expressed interest in learning to tell time? Has your child learned to tell time? • Does your child watch live television programming (indicating they may have a concept of time) or only streaming or prerecorded programming? If your child watches live programs, which ones? (Some educational programming exposes young people to the concept of time.)
Readiness	• What level of familiarity with time do students have? • How important and in what ways is telling time/time important in students' lives? • Are students aware of the features of timepieces?	Ask students: • Do you have clocks at home? If so, where? What kind (digital, analog, wristwatches, ones with Roman numerals)? • How is time used at your house? Do you have to get ready "on time" for school? Is there a particular time you eat meals or do other activities? How is time related to daylight? How do you know how much time passes? • How do you use time outside school?
Learning profile	• What parts of this standard might students struggle with?	Reflect on past learning: • Are there students who have difficulty with conceptual tasks? • Are there students who have difficulty with procedural tasks?

their learning, and inspire greater motivation for and attention to educational experiences.

Pre-assessments can function as "advanced organizers," engaging students intellectually with the material they will be learning. In a differentiated setting, they function to prepare all students for new learning and offer special support that promotes equity. A pre-assessment that introduces the material that will be learned can orient students to forthcoming facts, procedures, and concepts and help them prepare before learning takes place. This is especially helpful for students who may lack prior exposure to targeted content (e.g., geographic landforms, literary genres, sports, mathematical content) outside school, never fully understood it, or have a poor memory of its previous introduction. It can be particularly helpful to design pre-assessments in a way that links past and future learning. For example, a music teacher gearing up for a unit on jazz might design a pre-assessment that asks students to listen to samples of jazz and of folk music (the focus of an earlier unit), then compare and contrast them using a Venn diagram. Students respond to prompts asking them to consider the instruments, rhythms, and other features in the genre samples, making connections between past and new learning. Experiences like this help develop the supportive mental frameworks that facilitate future learning (i.e., *schemas*).

Support Student Involvement and Needs

In differentiated classrooms, teachers actively invite their students to be partners in the learning process. One of the ways to do this is by being transparent about the goals and purpose of the assigned activities. Pre-assessments can help you communicate the purpose for learning and invite students to participate in it. Pre-assessments also give students advanced notice about the goals and expectations for their learning and time to mentally prepare for it. For example, prior to a unit on forces, magnets, and motion, a teacher might ask students to read and define a list of important vocabulary words. Considering this content before they are expected to do anything with it (i.e., for a grade) provides a less intimidating entry to instruction. It also helps them become aware that the teacher wants to prepare them for new material. Allocating prep time communicates "this learning is important."

Students benefit from pre-assessment when their teachers design and implement responsive instruction based on the information generated. They also benefit when they are invited to cooperate with their teacher and offer input for instructional decision making (the principle of partnership). This participation prepares them for new learning and adds to their understanding of themselves. In differentiated settings, students are invited to consider what they do and do not know and asked to reflect on their present status as it relates to new learning. Participation in pre-assessment makes it a learning experience where students grow in self-awareness and the ability to practice self-analysis.

In well-run differentiated classrooms, students receive the support they need to be successful, and this extends to pre-assessment. If all students are going to be partners in the teaching–learning process, then teachers must ensure that the process is universally comprehensible and accessible. This means seeking the most accurate information about students' needs and assets. *Accurate information* truly represents student readiness, interest, and learning profile.

There are many factors that influence the accuracy of information gleaned from student assessments, including (1) the student's desire to provide information to the teacher through the assessment (sometimes they are unmotivated to do so and may not give their best or true effort), (2) the student's ability to read and comprehend questions, and (3) the student's ability to understand and correctly interpret the items on an assessment. There are ways teachers can increase the accuracy of information or data collected when developing assessments.

To design pre-assessments that yield more accurate information and are more equitable for students, first **identify your rationale for the pre-assessment and content you will include**. Write a short pre-assessment focusing on the information you need most. This way, you will not waste time and energy on information you will not or cannot use. Assessment items and questions that are well written and easy for your students to understand are more likely to yield accurate information. Using closed-ended questions rather than open ones will make it easier to interpret data.

Structure the content as needed for your students. Use familiar words when possible and define unfamiliar terms when appropriate so you will get the information you're seeking (even if students don't yet understand key terminology). Provide contextual support or coaching as needed. Use phrasing your learners will understand Avoid double negatives, vague or overly general questions, and leading questions that encourage students to choose a specific answer. Anticipate the answers you will receive and provide choices when possible (but don't make lists of choices too long). If you cannot think of the entire range of possible answers, include a category for "other."

Make students partners in the process and incorporate modifications that address students' needs. Make sure students know how the pre-assessment data will be used and why they should try their best. Assure them that you will be looking at the pre-assessment results not to issue grades but to help you design more effective instruction. For many students, sequencing questions from easier to increasing difficulty will make the pre-assessment more accessible. Are there other barriers that might prevent full participation from some students? If you have a student who would provide more accurate input sharing it verbally instead of textually, offer the option of recording responses in an audio file. Such practices foster a sense of community and inclusion and cultivate more equitable learning environments.

Finally, **revise your pre-assessments.** Analyze the data they generated and take stock before using them again. Did the questions you set elicit responses that supported valid conclusions about your students' pre-instruction status? Do you need to modify questions to ensure they generate more useful information about what and how to teach? Likewise, if the data you gather during instruction reveal other aspects of the learning sequence you didn't cover in the pre-assessment, go back and modify the pre-assessment instrument accordingly.

Using Digital Tools to Address the 4Es and Respond to Barriers

For pre-assessments to be equitable, they must respond to the needs of the many different learners in the classroom. This removes the barriers that might keep you from getting accurate information for instructional decisions. Further, digital tools address some of the barriers many teachers experience with pre-assessment and can save time and improve the utility of such inquiry. Digital tools can help you to (1) support student expression by using pedagogical technologies (e.g., brainstorming and concept mapping tools); (2) stimulate student interest and involvement (e.g., digital games); and (3) streamline the design, implementation, and analysis of pre-assessments.

Brainstorming and Concept Mapping Tools

Different students benefit from different materials and methods of pre-assessment. Digital tools have some affordances. They can stimulate and support the creative expression of students' existing knowledge because they allow students to more easily edit and save different versions of their work, as well as to incorporate graphics, video, and hyperlinks—a great use of them as a pedagogical technology. Students can also use these tools for brainstorming, drawing a flowchart, or creating a hierarchical representation of what they already know about the topic or topics they will be studying.

The brainstorming tools (e.g., charts, clip art, shapes) embedded within most word processing programs assist with ideation (i.e., the generation of ideas). These can be especially helpful when you want students to share factual knowledge (e.g., vocabulary, facts, key ideas), procedural knowledge (e.g., steps, methods), or other types of knowledge (see Chapter 7) related to an upcoming unit of study. Use of such tools can help students express their existing knowledge with more freedom and control. Selecting and completing the diagrams (e.g., cycles, hierarchies, processes, lists) built into tools such as Microsoft Word's SmartArt can free up insights buried below a student's conscious awareness.

Concept mapping tools available as software (e.g., Inspiration) and online (e.g., Bubbl.us, Gliffy, MindMup) are another helpful support when students are being pre-assessed. Although they can also be used for brainstorming, concept maps are a graphic organizer that represents ideas and their relationships. Different types of concept maps that students might create include the following (Kilbane & Milman, 2014):

- **Flowcharts** that use connecting lines to organize information in a procedural manner. Flowcharts show the sequence or order for completing a task, solving a problem, or implementing a systematic process of events.
- **Hierarchical maps** organize concepts in a hierarchical manner with the most important concept (the superordinate concept) on the top. Coordinate and subordinate concepts fall under the main, superordinate concept.
- **Pictorial maps** display items using graphics, pictures, or drawings. The emphasis is on the pictorial representation of the concepts.
- **Web, spider, bubble, or cluster maps**, although differing in appearance, all organize information about an important, central concept and position the subordinate concepts around it.

Concept maps make it possible for students to express an understanding of relationships between ideas through shapes and words. They are helpful if you want to gain an understanding of students' conceptual knowledge (e.g., recognition of general organizing constructions, mental structures, relationships), procedural knowledge (e.g., steps in a cycle), or factual knowledge (e.g., the relationships between various concepts or "big ideas" associated with learning). These tools allow a process of creation and expression that is different from communicating by writing in other formats (e.g., a short-answer essay or bulleted list). Although they are easy to use, one of their constraints is that they require special skills before students can use them efficiently and benefit from them fully.

Digital Games

Games have been used in classrooms to assess student learning, increase student motivation, and engage students in learning for years. Remember math relays, where the class was divided into two teams and a representative from each team came to the front of the room to answer a math problem? Many teachers like to use gaming or gamification for pre-assessment because it's usually something students enjoy. Games can help you gauge student readiness (especially foundational knowledge or existing mastery of upcoming material), interests, and learning profile.

They are also particularly good for assessing students' factual (e.g., vocabulary, terminology, rules, principles) and procedural knowledge (e.g., step-by-step ways of doing something, methods) because they lend themselves to short answers and objective questions.

With online game tools (e.g., JeopardyLabs, Kahoot!, Socrative), teachers input pre-assessment questions that students later access on computers, tablets, or other devices to compete against each other in a game-show format. Digital tools such as whiteboards can be used with presentation software (e.g., Keynote, SMART Notebook, PowerPoint, Canva) to create games from templates (e.g., Connect4, Family Feud). Integrating other digital tools like student response systems and online survey tools can make learning more fun and boost student investment. One constraint of digital games is because they are so engaging, they can direct attention toward the digital tools and competition and away from the people who should be at the heart of all learning experiences. Using them in moderation balances their affordances and constraints.

Operational Technologies

Operational technologies have many affordances that enable teachers to practice pre-assessment more easily and with greater impact. They can reduce the amount of time spent developing pre-assessment tools; used strategically, they can enhance teaching effectiveness.

Because digital tools make it easier to write and edit pre-assessment items, they enable more effective and equitable design. You can edit pre-assessments to improve future implementation or revise and reuse the same ones for other purposes and students. For younger learners, you can include images and other graphics that make it easier for them to interpret what is being asked and to provide an accurate response. Artificial intelligence tools (e.g., Adobe Firefly and Canva Magic Media) are helpful for generating images and graphics. With online survey tools or forms (e.g., Google Forms, SurveyMonkey, survey/testing tools embedded in learning management systems), you can select from various types of items (e.g., multiple choice, select multiple entries) and include images to help multilingual learners decode the written prompts inquiring about their understanding.

Digital tools can also make administering and analyzing pre-assessment easier and more efficient. Online survey tools can be accessed easily (provided networked devices are available during and outside of class time), offering new possibilities: Pre-assessment no longer needs to occur solely during class time. Digital distribution also saves the time required to make copies of, hand out, and collect paper assessments. Using digital tools, teachers can automatically organize and analyze the data they collect as graphs, charts, and tables. Tools like Edpuzzle, Nearpod, Zoho Show, and Pear Deck allow teachers to create pre-assessment presentations with questions embedded. These tools then track students' completion rates and scores, which teachers can review and analyze to determine the next steps for instruction. It is easier for teachers and students to see patterns in the data, resulting in easier recognition of individual and shared interests or needs. Some programs even offer multiple visual representations of the data, which allows teachers to choose the displays that are most helpful to their analysis and instructional decisions.

Questions for Reflection

- How and when do you use pre-assessment with your students?
- Of the digital tools you have used, which have been effective? What have you learned from using them, and which are most helpful for pre-assessment?
- What digital tools have you not previously considered but would like to try for pre-assessment? What are the pros and cons of using these digital tools?
- Which of the digital tools described in this chapter might help you collect and analyze data about your students' understanding of a unit of instruction?

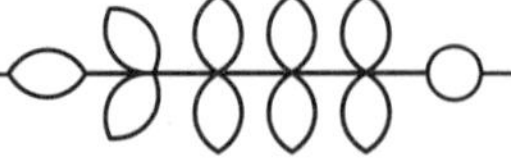

5

Designing and Using Different Types of Assessment

This chapter covers...

- The different types of assessment to use in a differentiated setting.
- The key practices that promote effective assessment.
- How to use digital tools to reduce barriers and address the 4Es during assessment.

As teachers gain experience, their ability to make strong instructional decisions improves. Over the years, they become more effective—but often only after a few years of seeing students struggle unproductively or fail to meet learning goals. Although learning across time and through trial and error is powerful, the negative impact this "slow approach" to professional development has on students must be acknowledged, especially when there are other methods for building instructional expertise. Chief among these is the strategic implementation of different types of assessment—the surest and quickest way for teachers to improve as instructional decision makers. The benefits for students are considerable as well.

What Is Assessment in a Differentiated Classroom?

Assessment describes a broad category of educational practices whose primary purpose is to acquire information related to student learning. In addition to pre-assessment (see Chapter 4), there is formative assessment, peer assessment, self-assessment, and summative assessment. Each type captures data that, when analyzed properly, generates valuable information about students: what they are learning, details about their progress (e.g., degree of ease, potential struggles), and the effect of the teacher's instructional decisions. Though alike in this way, each type of assessment is distinct in (1) the type of information it seeks to identify, (2) the timing of its implementation within the instructional process, (3) the methods for conducting it, and (4) its ability to promote noncurricular learning outcomes.

Pre-assessment

As discussed in Chapter 4, teachers pre-assess student mastery of targeted content and skills before developing instructional plans for a lesson, learning sequence, or unit. During pre-assessment, teachers also inquire to discover other details about their students—their background knowledge, past experience with the topic, interest in the topic—that is likely to affect how the students will approach the content. A secondary purpose of pre-assessment is to generate information about students' current, pre-instruction levels of knowledge and proficiency with the content in order to compare it with their post-instruction levels and document individual growth (Kilbane & Milman, 2014).

As noted in Chapter 4, pre-assessment and formative assessment (which we will focus on shortly) are linked, as both generate data used to inform instructional decisions. This makes both useful in differentiated classrooms, where teachers need to adjust the design for learning to respond to the unique students engaged in it. Carefully conceived and administered pre-assessments generate data that can be applied to guide beneficial educational design decisions. The main reason we treat pre-assessment separately in Chapter 4 is because it is such an important driver of effectively designed differentiation.

Formative Assessment

Formative assessment, as we define it, is instructional inquiry performed during the implementation of a lesson, learning sequence, or unit. Its primary purpose is to collect information about students' progress.

Formative assessment data can be gathered through a variety of means, including (1) teacher observation and one-on-one conferences with students; (2) quizzes, in-class responses to questions, checklists, and homework; and (3) reflective journaling, freewriting, and summary papers.

Gauging student progress *during* learning helps teachers gain a better understanding of the efficacy of their educational designs. Are the decisions they made about how to approach the content having the desired effect? In what ways, and for whom? It also provides useful information while there is still an opportunity to amend the instructional approach. Teachers can analyze this assessment data and adjust variables to mediate struggles students may be experiencing, increase challenges, and otherwise influence the quantity and quality of students' learning. Sharing progress data with students allows them to make parallel adjustments to their learning approach: they can read more closely, review their work, ask more questions, and so on.

Formative assessment is particularly important in a differentiated classroom, where providing students with accurately tailored scaffolds and supports is a priority. Data from formative assessment can help you determine (1) if and how well students understand the content; (2) whether and how to modify parts of the instructional process (e.g., where to adjust pacing, teaching method, student grouping arrangements, and materials in use) to better address the needs of specific learners; (3) how well your organizational procedures are working; (4) if and where content misconceptions exist; and (5) which concepts need to be readdressed or reinforced. Formative assessment also promotes other beneficial outcomes, such as cultivating students' metacognition, fostering student–teacher relationships, and enhancing satisfaction in the learning process (for both you and your students).

Self-assessment

Self-assessment is when the students themselves generate data about what and how well they are learning. The insights it produces benefits teachers and students alike.

Careful attention to the design and timing of self-assessment can increase its power. For example, students working to complete a lab experiment might benefit from a checklist-style self-assessment that details the important aspects of the work. As they check off each step in the experiment, they also respond to prompts asking them to note observed outcomes, reflect on the observations, synthesize the results, review the information in the textbook, note inconsistencies, and raise additional questions. Of course, teachers can monitor students' progress to see if, and the degree to which, they completed the different tasks linked to successful learning, but it's the students who stand to benefit the most. Asking them to complete this kind of self-assessment nudges them to engage more deeply in the learning process as they perform behaviors that will help them complete the assignment. If students are receptive, they may also begin to appreciate the many steps associated with deep learning and increase their metacognition, becoming more reflective, thoughtful, and independent learners.

Self-assessment can be implemented at any stage of the learning process—before, during, and after it takes place. You can ask students to assess what they already know about a topic or to identify their current level of skill before beginning a lesson, or to reflect on what they have learned or how much they have grown at the end of a unit. Prompts such as "What was this unit about? What was the most useful/meaningful thing you learned in this unit? What are some questions or concerns you still have regarding the topic we are studying?" can promote student self-reflection. Imagine the effects on students' metacognition if you ask them to self-assess at different stages throughout an entire learning experience!

In differentiated classrooms, where students and teachers function as partners in learning, self-assessment is a way to nudge students to learn about themselves as well as the content. It directs them to consider their behaviors and how they have responded to the demands set for them. For example, what talents and assets did they bring to the learning process in this unit? How did their talents and assets affect their success? What was challenging or difficult about the learning process in this unit? How did they respond to challenges and difficulties? Which strategies or mindset shifts were involved? What might they do differently in the future?

It is helpful to use a variety of self-assessment methods and modes because it provides a broader understanding of student learning, calls attention to students' different learning processes, and honors individual student variance. You might consider asking students to keep a journal to document their growth in learning over time, to collect digital snapshots of work products they are particularly proud of, or to reflect on items that are included in a cumulative portfolio. Regular self-assessment affirms for students just how important a factor they are in the educational process. It helps them develop self-awareness and greater facility with metacognition. They also gain a greater sense of agency, which is essential for developing as independent, lifelong learners.

Peer Assessment

Classroom learning is a social enterprise, and the interpersonal interactions that occur among members of such a community can be educationally powerful. This is certainly the case with peer assessment.

Reviewing and commenting on classmates' work, as well as reflecting on the feedback classmates provide on one's own work, enhances and expands the learning experience. Peer assessment often leads to immediate practical improvement, as students adjust products and processes in response to this outside input, but its greater power is the way it helps students build capacity over time. Through analyzing what their peers have produced, students gain insight into other ways they might approach their own acquisition of knowledge and skills. Peer assessment also expands students' learning by cultivating critical thinking and communication skills, such as when they apply an analytical framework to their peers' work products and come up with ways to talk about their progress. Regular involvement in well-managed peer assessment also improves students' ability to appraise products (both their own and those of others) and provides opportunities for them to learn to give different types of feedback—affirmations, reviews, and critiques.

Preparing students to engage in peer assessment is important, because each student varies in their readiness for this work. Teachers must explicitly explain the general goal of peer assessment (i.e., to give feedback that helps other students grow) and point out any other specific goals for its implementation in particular uses. Some teachers use the process to promote accountability and better student performance; they realize that impressing a peer who is evaluating their work can motivate certain students to work harder and with greater focus. Other teachers use peer assessment to provide students with learning experiences that complement their instruction. Because peers have more in common (e.g., vocabulary, life experiences, developmental stage), they can relate to and teach one another in ways a teacher cannot.

Preparing students to practice peer assessment requires ensuring that all the students recognize the significance of their investment in the process; they bear a powerful responsibility. Students will benefit from instruction on how to provide meaningful feedback and from practice fulfilling your expectations for their involvement. For example, you will want to distinguish whether the expectation of peer review is to critique, guide, or affirm their peer.

Peer assessment practices range from simple to complex. Reading and reacting to a peer's work with a simple written response may be sufficient practice if the goal is to promote individual accountability for following assignment guidelines and to motivate students to complete their work. Affixing sticky notes to a project that indicate its strong and weak attributes is appropriate if the goal is to improve a peer's work. If students apply the same rubric the teacher will use, their evaluation may point out areas where additional progress can be made before a final assessment is made and a grade determined. Depending on the context in which peer assessment is implemented, it may be desirable for it to be performed anonymously and without recognition of who is giving or receiving feedback on the work.

Peer assessment can be leveraged to strengthen connections and community among learners. When students review one another's work, they learn about one another and experience the joy and value of collaboration. Peer assessment can also empower students to take more responsibility for their own learning and that of their peers. Based on feedback received during the learning process, they can self-correct misconceptions they may have or refocus on effective learning processes.

When using peer assessment in differentiated classrooms, always consider students' unique skills and the class dynamics. This is a skill that can challenge all students, but younger ones in particular; as students advance through the grade levels, their developing content understandings and social skills tend to make for more detailed and valuable peer assessment. But inevitably, and independent of grade level, natural student variance means some will be more skilled and comfortable with providing and receiving peer feedback than others. Teachers must be prepared to provide developmentally appropriate instruction on giving constructive feedback to peers, along with scaffolding supports, such as rubrics and sentence stems.

Of course, some students will need considerable support to fully participate in the peer assessment process, and it's possible some students will not be able to engage in peer assessment to the degree that others will. In such cases, you may want to supplement planned peer assessment with self-assessment and teacher conferences.

Summative Assessment

Summative assessment occurs at the end of learning sequences and captures more conclusive information about student performance. It's a demonstration of what students know, understand, and are able to do as a result of instruction. Summative assessment should always be planned, intentional, and focused.

The two most popular types of summative assessment are performance tasks and learning products. **Performance tasks** are traditional measures of student learning (e.g., tests, quizzes, essays, lab reports). **Learning products** (or just *products* for short; see Chapter 8) involve some type of creative development and expression (e.g., a drawing, story, web page, infographic). Products differ from traditional performance tasks in that they are more open to student choice, more flexible, and can be more motivational or personal. They often require students to work at a broader or deeper level and frequently involve collaboration.

Both types of summative assessment are commonly implemented at the end of a substantial, extended learning experience (e.g., a learning sequence, unit, or term). However, they can be administered at any stage of the learning process when the goal is to make a definitive judgment (i.e., generate a letter grade) or to get a snapshot of a student's skill and knowledge status. Typically, what a teacher ascertains from summative assessments becomes the basis for a student's grade report, which are often communicated to family members. Sharing this information with the students also provides them with an opportunity to reflect on their achievement, growth, and effort.

Traditional summative assessments include tests and quizzes, sometimes offering students alternatives in responding via other media formats (e.g., audio recording, visual representations). **Authentic assessments** attempt to identify the depth, breadth, and other qualities associated with students' learning through a meaningful, practical, or real-life application of learning (e.g., podcasts, conversations).

In differentiated learning environments, where teachers strive to ensure that each student receives the support they need to learn and demonstrate their learning optimally, there are two powerful ways to adjust a summative assessment: by modifying the materials, tools, and environmental conditions that affect students' success and by offering students choice.

The **materials, tools, and environmental conditions** in your classroom each function in a unique way: they can either set students up to succeed, or not. For example, the materials used in an assessment can make it easier for a student to give an accurate representation of their learning or make it harder for them to provide such evidence. If assessment materials are poorly designed, hard to understand, or not well matched to learning targets, they can obscure what students have truly accomplished. The environmental support surrounding students as they engage with an assessment can help them perform better—or less well. A teacher's "pep talk" before an assessment might encourage and motivate some students to give their best effort and demotivate others, causing them anxiety that negatively affects their best performance.

As explained in Chapter 4, the aim of differentiating these aspects of an assessment is to remove the "noise" (i.e., negative influences) that makes the "signal" (i.e., student learning) harder to hear and communication of students' learning hard to recognize. For example, giving students a checklist of the steps involved in completing an assessment instead of just offering verbal instructions makes it easier for students to perform successfully—especially students who have difficulty remembering procedures or are prone to leaving work unfinished. Or, if your goal is to assess students' application skills rather than their retention skills, letting them use a glossary or calculator during a summative assessment can generate a truer picture of what you want to assess.

Offering students choices about the method they use to demonstrate their learning can be motivational, resulting in increased effort and better work. In addition, it allows students to select how to showcase their accomplishments. Many teachers use "choice menus" for a summative assessment. Like a menu at a restaurant, students select from a range of possibilities and choose their preferred method of displaying their skills and knowledge.

For example, for a 3rd grade class science unit,

- Students might choose (as an "appetizer") to demonstrate their understanding of vocabulary words relating to the water cycle by writing a definition, sharing it orally with their teacher, or drawing a graphic.
- For the "main course," they might demonstrate their knowledge of the specific steps and order of steps in the water cycle by writing a short essay, completing a drawing, or acting it out.
- Finally, for "dessert," students might share their awareness of the way people interact with water in the various stages of the water cycle by completing fill-in-the-blank sentences, writing an original play or story, or devising their own method (so long as it meets the requirements in a rubric).

In the differentiated classroom, each assessment type is distinct and important. Each provides a different data point to understand students' progress and the effect of modifications made for their benefit. However, assessment is also viewed as a whole: each type is complementary and works in a coordinated way to support the success of both teacher and students. For students, the use of different assessment types forms a reinforcing structure that is strategically integrated across their learning progress, offering focused support at critical moments of development.

Pre-assessment prepares students for the learning process and gives the teacher a better idea of how and where to start. Formative assessment serves as a "check-in" that enables opportunities for redirection and recalibration. Summative assessment provides recognition of success and a form of closure. Peer and self-assessments function to complement learning and create important connections. For teachers who differentiate effectively, assessment functions as a cycle: it provides information that directs decisions, incorporates points for recalibration, and offers opportunities to learn from past practice. Assessment flows throughout all aspects of instruction, enriching and providing teacher and students with the knowledge and experiences they need to thrive (see Figure 5.1).

Planning for Assessment in a Differentiated Classroom

To design a learning environment where assessments not only gauge learning but also promote it, you first need to develop a strategic plan for assessment. Articulating clear goals for what you hope to accomplish increases the likelihood of a good match between your goals for assessment and the means you use. This is, in effect, thinking about assessment with the mindset of an educational designer. Take a few moments to consider which types of assessment—formative, peer, self-, or summative—you might use to meet the following goals:

- Increase students' awareness of personal progress, growth, and achievement.
- Cultivate students' abilities to reflect on and learn from their experiences, fostering their capacity for independent, self-regulated learning.
- Promote students' ability to support their classmates' growth and accomplishment.
- Expose students to different methods, strategies, and personal styles that can be used when completing an assignment or learning task.
- Improve students' work while it is in progress.
- Refine student understanding of the content being studied and address misconceptions or errors before they become permanent.

We recommend developing a plan that employs different types of assessment over the course of a year, semester, or other portion of time.

FIGURE 5.1
The Flow of Instruction in a Differentiated Classroom

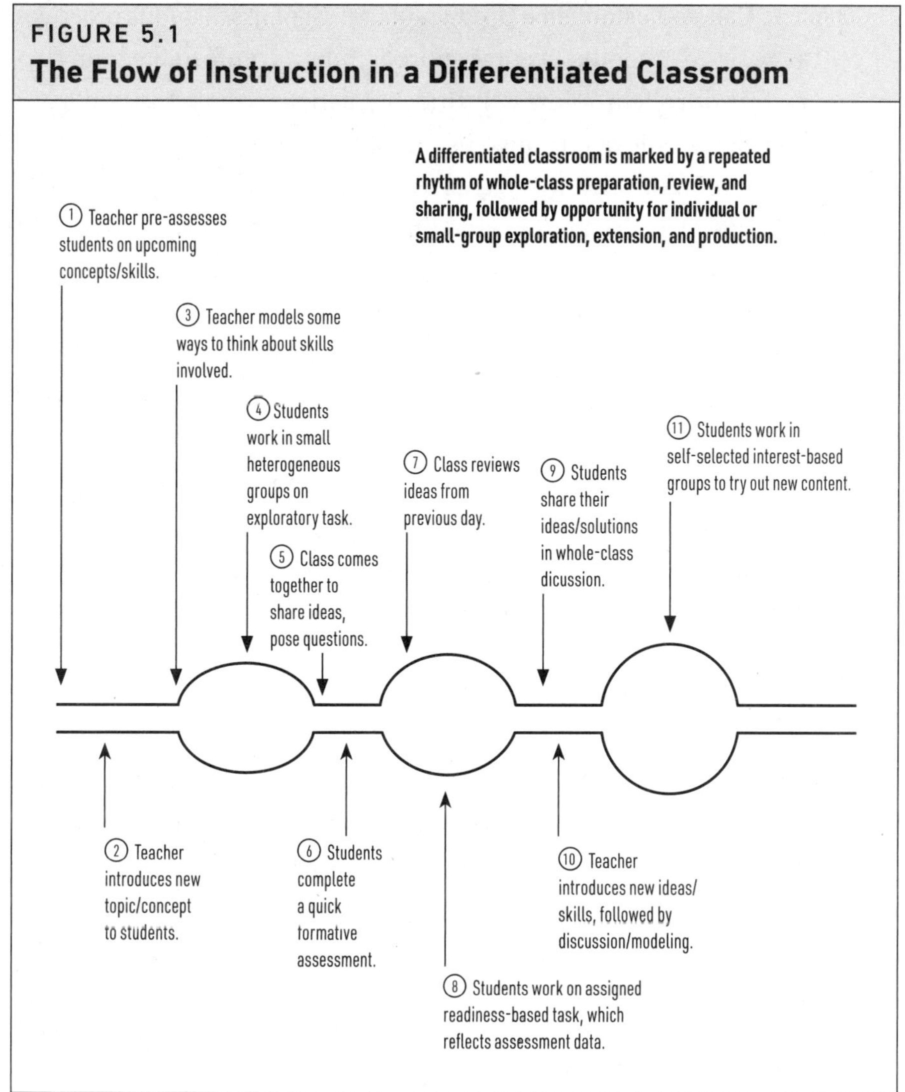

Source: From *How to Differentiate Instruction in Academically Diverse Classrooms* (3rd ed.), p. 9, by C. A. Tomlinson, 2017. Copyright © 2017 ASCD.

Determining how often to use each type, what methods will work best, and how to integrate the methods in order to generate the best data for yourself and students will increase the impact of these regular practices.

To develop an assessment plan, follow these steps:

1. **Identify your priorities** for each type of assessment—formative, peer, self-, and summative—and roughly how often you want to use

each. Can you establish a predictable range of assessment practices that ensure students become more familiar, comfortable, and successful with them? How will students benefit from what you learn and what they learn through using these assessments?

2. **Design consistent messages** to communicate the purpose for each type of assessment to students and their families. Do you want to emphasize the benefits to both teacher and students? Or emphasize how they promote growth and independent learning in addition to providing information for the teacher's benefit? Are there ways to invite communication and appreciation for these practices from families?
3. **Identify how you will offer choice** (when possible) within the various assessment practices you want to use.
4. **Identify measures to ensure students' well-being** and emotional safety. Do you want to implement "blind" peer assessments to promote confidentiality? "Blind" summative assessments to prevent possible teacher bias?
5. **Choose tools and technologies** to assist in implementing, analyzing, and applying assessment data. How will you ensure that these are appropriate for your students and convey the best data possible?
6. **Specify how you will use assessment data** for planning lessons, units, and other instruction. How will what you learn allow you to curate better resources, materials, and tools to support their learning? What changes might be needed based on what you learn from each type of assessment about student readiness, interest, and learning profile? How will this knowledge support modifying the content, process, products, and environments associated with instruction? As the year progresses, how will you refine your inquiry with each type of assessment based on what you are learning?

And, finally, ask yourself how you'll use what you learn from this year's students to refine your professional expertise moving forward.

It can also be helpful to consider goals for specific assessments—to ensure that each is best able to fulfill its purpose. The preceding questions can be applied to individual, specific assessments, helping you refine your goals for each (e.g., focusing on student readiness, interest, or learning profile—or a combination). When designing specific assessments, also consider how each might promote students' learning about themselves. You might ask students to reflect on the data generated after you have looked at it, or to include results in a portfolio that records information about their learning needs and interests. With each assessment, consider, too, how you might apply the data it will generate to strengthen classroom relationships, affirm the value of each student, and promote self-awareness and independent learning.

Key Practices for Effective Assessment

When implemented regularly and strategically, assessment can make learning more successful for each student, enrich relationships, and boost teacher efficacy and fulfillment. The complication is that it's challenging to design truly effective assessments—ones that address standards, goals, and objectives while also providing meaningful information about students' learning and your instructional approach. Fortunately, there are powerful assessment practices that can help teachers maximize the benefits of various assessment types.

Key practices that educational designers should have in their skill set include (1) differentiating assessments; (2) ensuring alignment between objectives, instruction, and assessments; and (3) involving students in developing assessments and analyzing assessment outcomes.

Differentiate the Assessments

Assessments can be differentiated—through low- and high-tech approaches—to support key aspects of student readiness, interest, and learning profile. Rotating between a predictable variety of formats (e.g., exit tickets, journaling, quizzes, rubrics), provided they all are effective, means that students do not become bored or complacent. Digital tools have many affordances for assessment: they can increase student interest and engagement, have features (e.g., annotation, screen overlays) that support more precise analysis, and enable archiving versions to assist comparison. There are some constraints, however, in ease of use and logistical deployment.

As previously mentioned, you also can engage students in differentiating assessments by giving them options for demonstrating their learning or asking them to develop assessments for themselves. You could ask groups of students to work together to identify questions that might appear on their end-of-unit test, then select the best ones to include. Other questions can help you identify areas where further refinement of knowledge might be needed before testing. Bear in mind that one size does not fit all; the assessments you (or your students) create should reflect this.

Align Objectives, Instruction, and Assessments

One of the most important aspects involved in designing effective assessment is ensuring alignment between objectives, instruction, and assessment. It should be clear from the assessment what is being measured and how. The assessment also should reflect how the content was taught. For instance, if an objective is for students to demonstrate calculations using a graphing calculator in a math course, then a performance-based assessment would be more appropriate than a multiple-choice assessment. Such an assessment might require students to create a video of the steps they completed to do the calculations while also explaining why.

Collaborate with Students

It is important for teachers to involve students in creating assessments, when possible—and this can be accomplished in a variety of ways. Teachers can create assessments and ask students for feedback that improves them. Students can also develop assessments for their peers, critique assessments created by you, or critique an AI-generated assessment. Collaborating with students includes sharing with them their results so they, too, can analyze these and better determine the next steps for their learning. They might recognize gaps in their learning or identify areas of the content that are challenging and where they need more targeted practice. Such feedback should be provided as soon as possible after assessment, so students do not struggle to make connections with what they learned and the feedback.

Using Digital Tools to Address the 4Es and Respond to Barriers

Assessments are not just for evaluating student progress; they also contribute to students' growth as individuals and development as independent learners. Digital tools can help (1) facilitate personal connections in the assessment process, (2) increase the clarity and depth of feedback, (3) archive and edit assessments, and (4) enable analysis and recognition of growth.

Facilitate Personal Connections

The personal relationships within the differentiated learning environment are a powerful, often unrecognized force that influences students' feelings about school as a community, their learning, and their growth. Attention and encouragement from teachers and peers inspire students to persevere when tasks get challenging and motivate them to invest in their work and strive for increasing excellence. Conversely, a lack of personal connection can have a negative effect on students, and in the assessment process, it can result in students feeling like an object being appraised ("What is my worth?") rather than a person whose value is not contingent upon their productivity and academic output. The assessments you design should balance students' needs for connection and affirmation with the truthful, accurate feedback they require for growth.

It can be beneficial to provide minilessons on giving and receiving feedback. After all, participation in assessment—before, during, or after learning occurs—puts students in a vulnerable position, with their abilities and efforts on display. Any assessor (teacher or student) must be sensitive to this vulnerability. Whether it's numbers on a rubric or constructive comments written on an assignment, even a supportive appraisal can be uncomfortable for some students; feedback perceived as criticism can feel much worse. Remember: because the assessment process is inherently a personal process, it must be responsive to students in a personal way and built on a positive relationship that nurtures care and concern.

Using digital tools to capture and communicate assessment feedback in an audio or video format is one way to help the process feel more personal.

Many teachers can and do provide vivid and useful written feedback on their students' work, but there is an inimitable immediacy to responses that students can see and hear.

Any audio and video feedback should begin by calling a student by name and recognizing their efforts and the work's positive aspects. Next, move into a more detailed appraisal focused on areas for growth, and then conclude with enthusiastic encouragement, conveying confidence in students' potential. Audio and video feedback has the additional affordance of being easier for young learners to understand and promoting equity for those who struggle with print (e.g., beginning readers, students with dyslexia or low vision). Recorded feedback can also be efficient; however, it should not be used as a replacement for in-person interactions, which should remain a priority.

There are many different tools that capture audio and video feedback. Teachers can record student feedback with a small digital voice recorder that makes it easy to upload audio files and distribute them through a learning management system (e.g., Google Classroom, Canvas). Alternatively, teachers can use the recording feature on a smartphone and then transfer the files to their students' computers. Regardless of the method chosen for recording and sharing the files, it should be understood that it is important that all students are held accountable for reviewing the feedback and asking questions if they arise.

Incorporating a digital component into assessment practices can also "depersonalize" feedback in a constructive way. By that, we mean it provides a way to address and possibly alleviate some of the vulnerability that a student may experience when giving and receiving feedback, as well as some of the awkwardness that might accompany providing feedback to peers. If students' work—whether it's their product or performance or feedback they are offering on another's product or performance—is submitted in a digital format (e.g., if it is typed rather than handwritten), this adds a degree of anonymity that can be comforting. For example, when peer assessment is being used to evaluate a first draft of an essay, assurance that everyone's work will be reviewed anonymously so that no one will know the identity of the writer can help make the feedback feel more objective and less personal. Likewise, a peer reviewer can find it easier to offer honest, constructive feedback if they know their identity will not be revealed.

Increase the Clarity and Depth of Feedback

Formative assessment-based feedback is most likely to be effective when students understand it and have time to adjust their learning approach or change their behavior before they are assessed again. Effective feedback is "clear, purposeful, meaningful, and compatible with students' prior knowledge and... provide[s] logical connections" (Hattie & Timperly, 2007, p. 104). Digital tools can make feedback provided in assessments more effective in a number of different ways.

Digital tools can increase the clarity of the feedback by making it more specific. For example, when student work is in an electronic format, you can annotate or drop in comments exactly where you want to point out an issue or praise and reinforce a student's work. In many documents, including PDFs, sticky notes can be used to annotate or "talk to a text." Reviewing tools in word processors enable tracking changes in addition to accommodating reviewer comments.

Another affordance that digital tools offer is increasing the level of depth offered in feedback. This is especially important with formative assessment when work benefits from information about where and how to improve it. When providing a review of an assignment, for example, you can insert hyperlinks into the work and refer students to additional, helpful resources (e.g., a glossary, an animation, instructions that might have been overlooked). With some screen-casting tools (e.g., Camtasia, TechSmith Capture, Zoom), you can even overlay visual animations on a students' work.

Archive and Edit Assessments

When an assessment's directions, structure, or language is unclear or confusing to students, there's a risk they will respond in ways that misrepresent what they know and can do. Any assessment that fails to provide an accurate reflection of what students have learned relative to the intended KUDs is a failure, and any conclusions teachers draw from such an assessment will be invalid. The situation is compounded by the fact that problems with an assessment's structure and language typically come to light only after its implementation—when (and if) the teacher makes the effort to analyze why so many students got certain items wrong or responded in ways that the teacher did not intend.

This is an area where digital tools can definitely help. It's easy and quick to edit assessments developed in an electronic format, which in turn expedites their revision and improvement over time. In some cases, teachers can retest students on the revised items to gain more accurate assessment data.

Digital tools can be especially helpful for teachers who differentiate instruction, as they make it easy to tailor assessments in response to individual needs. A student who is learning to speak in a new language may need some definitions for academic language included in their version of an assessment; when the assessment is electronically developed and presented, this modification is easier to do. Likewise, with a digitally presented assessment, a student with limited vision or dyslexia could opt to have the text read aloud to them on headphones. Still another example is offering students different options for demonstrating mastery of the same set of identified learning goals; teachers might, for example, encourage students to choose whether they would like to create a multimedia presentation, write and perform a skit, or write a traditional research paper about a topic. The KUDs assessed would be the same, but the product would be differentiated based on learning profile.

Enable Analysis and Recognition of Growth

Effective assessments measure growth as well as achievement. Growth is only visible when comparing achievement at different stages of a student's development; this is an important practice in a differentiated learning environment, where it's understood that each student will have a unique trajectory. Learning is a long-term process, and all students will progress in the same direction... just at their own pace. Digital tools can be invaluable in the archiving of work in a way that promotes ready comparison and reflection.

Portfolios have been used in education for decades as performance-based assessments documenting students' learning over time. A portfolio is "a goal-driven, organized collection of artifacts that demonstrate [students'] knowledge and skills over time" (Kilbane & Milman, 2003, p. 4). Using digital portfolios provides numerous benefits, from the ability to document and share students' learning over time (including year-to-year and subject-to-subject) to promoting self-analysis and taking stock of what they have learned and reflecting on their progress and learning.

Different types of portfolios exist (e.g., developmental, showcase, thematic), and many different types of tools can be used to create them, from slide-development software (e.g., Google Slides, PowerPoint) to web development tools (e.g., Weebly) and turnkey solutions (e.g., bulb, ClassDojo, PortfolioGen) where students can create, house, and share their digital portfolios in a protected environment. For example, students might create a thematic portfolio focusing on the theme of growth that shows what and how they have learned particular content over the academic year. They might incorporate graphics or pictures that have trees in various stages of growth and different examples of their work to show how their learning has developed and grown over time.

Questions for Reflection

- How and when do you conduct pre-assessment, formative assessment, and summative assessment of your students?
- Do your assessments help you develop a better understanding of your students' knowledge, interests, and learning profiles? How so?
- What digital tools could you use for data collection and analysis? To differentiate assessments? To support students' self-assessment of their progress?

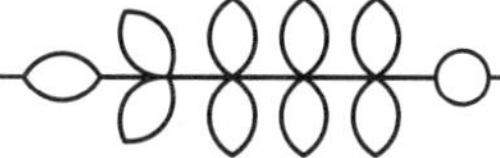

6

Differentiating Content

This chapter covers...

- How pedagogical, curricular, and content knowledge interact.
- The meaning and purpose of universal design for learning and culturally responsive teaching.
- The key design practices that support more successful content differentiation.
- How to use digital tools to reduce barriers and address the 4Es when differentiating content.

There are many aspects of the instructional process that can capture students' attention and motivate them to invest in the hard work of learning, but the content—the topics, ideas, and phenomena being studied—is usually what they find most inspiring.

Each academic discipline offers learners distinct ways to develop a deeper understanding of the world. Teachers who are already passionate about the content they teach delight in sharing its richness with students. However, because each student is one of a kind—with a unique personality, perception, background, and history—teachers must adjust for these variations when considering the content of instruction.

The point of differentiating content is to enable each student to engage more easily and fully with what is being studied. You can do this by consciously addressing student readiness, interests, and learning profile in your design for learning, which requires a broad and deep understanding of curriculum content and students as well as the pedagogical know-how necessary to ensure accessibility.

What Is Content?

Although common in K–12 settings, the term *content* is often used imprecisely. We define *content* as what teachers teach and what students endeavor to learn during a lesson, unit, or other educational experience. Teachers identify content when they define learning goals, instructional objectives, or KUDs (i.e., what students should know, understand, and be able to do). All of these communicate the content being studied, using phrases that articulate the expectations required for student mastery.

When differentiating instruction, it's helpful to think of content as the object or input that students gain exposure to through engagement with instructional experiences (like lectures) and materials. The learning process (see Chapter 7) allows students to make sense of and appropriate this content. For example, students studying the content of cell division or meiosis engage with the content as they read a textbook and study a diagram outlining the general phases. During the learning process, they ask questions and replicate the diagram of stages as a way to comprehend cell division. Although the content of learning and the process associated with it may be difficult to distinguish in practice, when designing for differentiation, it is helpful to think of them as separate instructional components that can be adjusted to promote student success.

The Importance of Professional Knowledge

Although it is important for educators to be proficient in the content they teach, proficiency is insufficient for effective differentiation. To differentiate well, teachers need *pedagogical content knowledge*—a deeper, more dynamic type of professional knowledge of the curriculum, the discipline it's drawn from, and how to teach it (Shulman, 1986). It's this complex professional knowledge they apply when deciding when, why, and how to make instructional modifications for individuals and groups of learners.

Pedagogical Knowledge

Pedagogical knowledge is a type of professional knowledge that teachers have about how to teach subject matter and how to make it comprehensible to students with different backgrounds, conceptions, and preconceptions. Derived from both "research [and] wisdom of practice" (Shulman, 1986, p. 9), pedagogical knowledge combines a theoretical and practical understanding of how people learn. For instance, elementary teachers might demonstrate their pedagogical knowledge by planning lessons that are developmentally appropriate (applying learning theories relevant to their students' age levels) and that involve practical strategies they have learned work best with their students.

Content Knowledge

Per Bruner (as cited in Shulman, 1992), *content knowledge* refers to a teacher's comprehension of the structure of knowledge in a particular academic discipline. It includes the theories, principles, and concepts of the discipline, as well as the facts and procedures associated with these. For example, math teachers with content knowledge of triangles know the theories that explain what triangles are, the basic facts expressing the properties or features of triangles (e.g., base, angles), the procedures for using them (e.g., as tools to create vertical and angled lines), and the concepts associated with them across different cases (e.g., right triangles, isosceles triangles). In a geometry class, some of the components of content knowledge students would learn include (1) theories (e.g., Pythagorean theorem), (2) principles (e.g., the sum of the lengths of any two sides of a triangle always exceeds the length of the third side), (3) concepts (e.g., "equal," "similar," "proportional"), facts (e.g., a polygon has three edges and three vertices), and procedures (e.g., how to calculate the height of a building).

There are also different aspects of the content, some of which (e.g., facts) may be more easily comprehensible for particular students, and more difficult (e.g., procedures) for others. Concepts (e.g., systems) often present challenges to students because they are more abstract and nuanced. There are special instructional models designed for teaching concepts, such as the concept attainment model, concept development model, and the inductive model (Kilbane & Milman, 2014), that include embedded supports for learner differences related to this content.

Teachers' experiences learning the content of a discipline—both during their initial schooling and later via their professional education—contribute to their development of content knowledge. Certain experiences are especially helpful, such as those that allow teachers to recognize the most powerful means for representing or communicating content (e.g., graphic organizers, animations, text). The study of their discipline helps them appreciate and point out for their students what might be interesting, memorable, or relevant about certain topics (e.g., that the structural strength used in triangles in the Great Pyramid of Giza allowed it to stand as the tallest human-made structure for 3,800 years).

When teachers have mastered the theories, principles, and practices associated with their subject, they are more likely to recognize what is difficult to comprehend (e.g., because of its abstractness or complexity) and provide appropriately differentiated support. They can also more easily identify where misunderstandings are likely or which details could be confusing.

In short: content knowledge is a valuable asset for a teacher who differentiates instruction. Intentionally reflecting on your own learning journey with various kinds of content can yield insights that are helpful when designing instructional experiences for your students.

Curricular Knowledge

According to Shulman (1986), *curricular knowledge* is what teachers know about the curriculum, and this consists of both "lateral" and "vertical" curricular knowledge (p. 10). *Lateral curricular knowledge* is a teacher's understanding of how the content relates to other subjects areas (e.g., math, science, social studies), and *vertical curricular knowledge* is the teacher's understanding of how the content fits within a larger sequence (e.g., what has been taught before and what will be taught in the future). Curricular knowledge includes (1) a recognition of how a particular segment of the curriculum is sequenced and relates to those before and after it, (2) knowledge of the range of approved curricular programs that might be used (e.g., text series, courses), (3) associated philosophical approaches (e.g., phonics, whole language), and (4) appropriate teaching materials (e.g., text, video, other resources).

The deeper and more varied your curricular knowledge, the more options you have when it comes to addressing content in your design for learning. For example, in 3rd grade language arts, curricular knowledge might encompass the following:

- Awareness of the horizontal course of study used for this grade level, the various strands within it, (e.g., reading, writing, speaking, listening), and the subcategories of each strand (e.g., reading: literature, key ideas and textual support, structural elements, organization).
- Recognition of how this content is vertically related to the foundational learning students experienced in 2nd grade and the learning they will perform in 4th grade.
- Recognition of the specific resources (e.g., texts, series, programs) approved for their use and an awareness of which would be most appropriate for using in their classroom, given the unique characteristics of their students and environment (e.g., physical space, class size).

Whether in a professional preparation program or paid employment, what teachers understand about the curriculum they are addressing with their students contributes significantly to their instructional efficacy.

Your curricular knowledge can help you appreciate how the new content you are presenting relates to what your students have already studied, which helps you partner with them more effectively to build strong networks of meaning. For example, a science teacher who knows that students have already studied cycles (e.g., the water cycle) can more easily help students recognize similarities and differences when learning about animal and human life cycles. This might lead the teacher to differentiate the content materials to include visuals (like those used when the students learned about the water cycle) to emphasize the cyclical nature of animal development.

Curricular knowledge can also help a teacher identify where gaps exist in students' foundational knowledge. The science teacher gearing up to teach animal and human life cycles might focus a pre-assessment (see Chapter 4) on the necessary building blocks of that unit's learning goals. If the resulting data reveals, for example, that a subset of the class does not understand what "cycles" are, this teacher would need to teach a supplementary minilesson on cycles to fill in the missing understanding.

Integrating Components of Professional Knowledge

In differentiated classrooms, teachers integrate the various components of their professional knowledge and their knowledge of their students to make decisions about which strategies to use when presenting content. When incorporating technology into their teaching and students' learning, they also apply TPACK, which is a type of professional knowledge about how to integrate technology in the teaching–learning process (see Figure 2.1, p. 20).

The goal of content differentiation is to make the experiences (e.g., lectures, presentations) and materials that communicate content (e.g., texts, videos) more accessible to all students. The term *accessible* suggests how content differentiation (1) makes the content easier to get into (e.g., more stimulating because it is interesting or relevant) and (2) makes the experiences and materials easier to reach (e.g., by removing unnecessary barriers to comprehension). Both are important when designing to effectively differentiate content.

Content differentiation does not lower standards or expectations for all or even some students. Instead, it ensures that the principles, concepts, procedures, and facts being studied will be encountered in a way that is equitable, providing for each student what is needed for full engagement and maximum participation. Effective content differentiation means that every learner has what they need to gain access to rich, meaningful content without unnecessary challenges.

To differentiate content, you need to take a multifaceted approach. Begin by incorporating standard practices that proactively establish that equitable conditions are the norm. These include the frequent use of formative assessment (see Chapter 5) to monitor student progress and intervene before struggles ensue and regular incorporation of choice (see Chapter 7) to empower students to select the resources and methods most supportive of their success. You also need to routinely offer content at varied levels of difficulty, building on Vygotsky's (1978) zone of proximal development (i.e., learning conditions where a student experiences the right amount of challenge and support for their optimal growth). With a foundation of these practices, you can then integrate other practices and digital tools in ways that further adjust for students' differences in readiness, interest, and learning profile.

Frameworks for Differentiating Content

More powerful differentiation—learning designs that lead more students to greater success—is possible when teachers begin from a foundation of good practice and strive for equity and inclusion. Two professional frameworks, **universal design for learning** and **culturally responsive teaching**, are compatible with differentiated instruction and offer complementary suggestions for effectively supporting students' differences. Both are useful in shaping an educational designer mindset.

Universal Design for Learning

Universal design for learning (UDL) is an education framework that applies principles from architectural design to learning. The goal behind the widespread use of certain architectural features (e.g., ramps, wide doors, tactile pavement) and fixtures (e.g., door levers, flat light switches)—namely, making buildings and other physical spaces more universally accessible to all people through more thoughtful, intentional design—serves as the inspiration for UDL. Developed by CAST (previously known as the Center for Applied Special Technology) in 1984 to support students with disabilities, UDL's focus is "to improve and optimize teaching and learning for all people based on scientific insights into how humans learn" (CAST, 2024, para. 1). The UDL framework identifies three aspects of the learning process that you should recognize and plan for when aiming to make learning accessible to all students: engagement, representation, and action and expression:

- **Engagement** refers to what stimulates or motivates a student to learn. To promote engagement, offer students choices as to the content materials they use or vary the levels of difficulty associated with learning about a topic.
- **Representation** is how the content is expressed and perceived or comprehended by the learner. In practice, this means providing content using a variety or combination of media (e.g., audio, print, video).

- **Action and expression** are how students indicate they have learned desired content. To differentiate this aspect of the learning process, vary the products students create to demonstrate what they have learned.

Traditional print text has been and continues to be one of the most popular choices for curriculum materials in classrooms. There are many reasons for this, ranging from its existing availability in schools (e.g., textbooks, library materials) to the fact that sharing and using it requires little technical expertise. Digital text has some advantages for making the content more equitable and accessible. Unlike print text, digital text enables the facts, concepts, and principles it contains to be communicated using various channels that remove barriers present when (1) students have visual impairments (e.g., low vision, blindness), (2) students struggle to read in general (e.g., little readiness, dyslexia), and (3) students struggle to comprehend in the language of the text (i.e., multilingual learners). Assistive technologies such as text readers can be easily employed to mitigate these barriers.

Effective ways to differentiate content include making audio recordings of print handouts, worksheets, and other teacher-created materials. By communicating text-based content through methods learners comprehend, teachers deliver content effectively and remove potential barriers. Using open-source texts and content (e.g., OERCommons) saves money while also providing more accessibility in many cases. Technology tools like digital text can help increase the accessibility of content to all students, as well as free up time for you to concentrate on more meaningful learning and tasks. There are many strategies for incorporating the use of digital text (see Figure 6.1).

Students benefit when they can use technology to support their viewing, sharing, and engagement with content, but be sure that your tech integration does not present new barriers to access. To ensure the technology you choose is accessible to the greatest number of students possible, bear in mind the "5As" of technology—availability, affordability, awareness, abilities, and agency (Roberts & Hernandez, 2019; see Chapter 2)—and be sure to weigh affordances and contraints.

FIGURE 6.1
Digital Text Features That Support Content Differentiation

Feature	Benefits
Change how the text looks on the screen	Meets user preferences for font (e.g., type, size, color); supports those who are visually challenged
Electronic highlighter	Points out key words, themes, characterizations, main ideas
Computer-generated summaries	Teachers or learners can create summaries that identify essential content
Check readability of selected text	Allows teachers and learners to select more appropriate reading materials
Integrated thesaurus or dictionary	Provides scaffolding of learners through difficult content and promotes comprehension
Text to speech	Reads individual words, phrases, sentences, or whole passages; some applications highlight each word as read it is so that students can follow along, increasing comprehension and reading skills

Culturally Responsive Teaching

Culturally responsive teaching (Gay, 2018, 2023) embraces students' cultural diversity and seeks to incorporate it to foster all students' academic success. It recognizes that culture is intertwined in teaching and learning and in the teaching–learning process. Embracing the principles of culturally responsive teaching can assist teachers in differentiating instruction more inclusively and successfully:

- Teachers should design instruction that **validates and affirms** their students' backgrounds by acknowledging individual heritages.
- Culturally responsive teaching is **comprehensive and inclusive**, focusing on the whole individual. Teachers should consider how instruction affects students cognitively, socially, psychologically, and physically, among other dimensions.

- Teachers who use culturally responsive teaching should plan **multidimensional instruction** that provides students with varied perspectives, media, and strategies for understanding the content.
- Culturally responsive teaching should **empower students**, helping them achieve academic success, increase their self-confidence, and improve the world around them.
- Culturally responsive teaching is **transformative**. It builds on a student's cultural background and academic strengths, resulting in a positive transformation of consciousness.
- Culturally responsive teaching **liberates learners** from the idea that there is only one truth or one way to do things. It offers a sense of freedom through "cooperation, community, and connectedness" (Gay, 2018, p. 36).
- Culturally responsive teaching is **humanistic**, cultivating students' comprehension of and an appreciation for themselves, their communities, the world, the diversity inherent in all of these, and respect for this diversity.
- Culturally responsive teaching is **normative and ethical**, involving understanding how culture affects teaching and learning and integrating cultural diversity in the teaching–learning process.

Culturally responsive teaching is very compatible with differentiation and a useful framework for understanding and improving practice. Culturally responsive teachers and those who differentiate instruction share a belief that diversity is natural, positive, and important to the experience of learning. They view cultural diversity as a source for enriching and expanding what is learned when it can be incorporated in the learning experience. Further, they understand how recognizing and supporting culturally diverse learners is important to building a classroom community (see Chapter 3).

Within the framework of differentiated instruction, consider how your students' cultural backgrounds might contribute to their learning profile and reflect on how you might affirm what they know and value in the content you teach. How might students' backgrounds and culture benefit and empower them in their present study, and what is the best way to respond as an educational designer who works in the service of these students?

In other words, given your students' cultural backgrounds, how can you introduce new content in a manner to maximize its appeal and relevance to them?

The frameworks of differentiation, UDL, and culturally responsive teaching were originally developed to provide focused support for specific groups of students (i.e., differentiated instruction grew out of support for gifted students; UDL from support for students with disabilities; culturally responsive teaching from support for a culturally diverse student body). Although their inspiration came from different sources, the goal of each is the same: supporting every learner so they feel valued and experience optimal success.

Key Practices for Differentiating Content

There are so many ways to differentiate content that it's impossible to list, let alone *describe*, them all. We are focusing here on several key practices that are particularly powerful across grade levels, subject areas, and settings, and worth adding to any educator's skill set: (1) offering multiple entry points, (2) using different types of presentations or "flipped" learning, (3) providing just-in-time support through ready resources, and (4) matching content with the most powerful medium. Practices that universally support all learners in every learning experience should be used as often as possible. Other practices are uniquely suited to supporting certain learners and should be integrated when needed as a response to information about student readiness or interest.

Provide Multiple Entry Points

Planning units, lessons, or learning sequences so that they have multiple entry points (i.e., a variety of avenues from which to enter instruction) is important and consistent with differentiation, UDL, and culturally responsive teaching. This practice ensures that the content is presented in a way that is most likely to interest learners and capture their attention. There are five distinct entry points to consider (Gardner, 1999) when designing compelling learning sequences and different ways to begin engagement with the content (see Figure 6.2).

FIGURE 6.2

Entry Points for Differentiating Content: An Overview

Entry Point	Description	Design Considerations
Aesthetic	Encourages learners to respond to formal and sensory qualities of content	• What are the sensory aspects related to this content that will be most intriguing for the students? • What is beautiful? Striking? • How can I make these aspects more perceivable and accessible in my presentation and engage students with the content?
Narrative	Provides storytelling elements related to content being studied	• What stories can I tell about the content—my own stories or those of others—that communicate the importance of this learning, its challenges, and its associated humor? • What might be interesting or funny to highlight?
Logical/ quantitative	Offers students an opportunity to respond to aspects that invite deductive reasoning or numerical consideration	• What logical understandings are related to this content? • Are there understandings quantified by data that students would find interesting and increase its relevance?
Foundational	Presents the broader concepts or philosophical issues related to content being studied	• What are the foundational concepts or principles related to this content? • How do students understand these in relation to the new content? • How can I bring these to the students' recognition to frame their learning?
Experiential	Invites students to respond to the content by doing something with their hands or bodies	• What experiences or ways to engage students' bodies will enable them to enter into a cognitive appreciation for the content and its relevance to them?

Vary Presentations and Flip Learning

There is a wide range of digital tools (e.g., Google Slides, Microsoft PowerPoint, Prezi) you can use to create multimedia presentations in support of instruction. By offering varied means of representing content, these tools expand your options for student engagement. In a single presentation, you might introduce students to the facts, principles, and processes associated with the content using text, outlines, diagrams, animations, audio, and video. Multimedia presentations also offer the affordance of integrating pre-assessment, formative assessment, and summative assessments. You can record a presentation as you teach, then save it for students who were absent or others who would benefit from a second or third view.

The specific content and method for accessing it in multimedia presentations can be differentiated for individual students or small groups based on their readiness, interest, or learning profile. You might create one version of the presentation for learners who are ready for the content at a basic level, another for those who are interested in more depth and rigor, and a third that offers support for concepts and vocabulary through hyperlinks and the insertion of additional slides containing related, foundational content.

Another method of differentiating content using multimedia involves using "flipped" learning, which is

> a pedagogical approach in which direct instruction moves from the group learning space to the individual learning space, and the resulting group space is transformed into a dynamic, interactive, learning environment where the educator guides students as they apply concepts and engage creatively in the subject matter. (Flipped Learning Network (2014, para. 4)

Flipped learning promotes active learning and problem solving while offering in-class support from the teacher. When using this method, include "check your understanding" questions in the presentation to ensure that students have experienced (e.g., watched, listened, or otherwise engaged with) and comprehend the presentation's content before they attempt to apply this learning. Questions can be embedded to ensure students' readiness for the content using different interactive video lesson platforms (e.g.,

Edpuzzle, Nearpod, Pear Deck, Zoho Show). Similarly, you might incorporate questions for assessment purposes or to scaffold student comprehension of the content.

Provide Just-in-Time Support

Different students benefit from different support when working to read, analyze, remember, and comprehend written materials. Presenting content in digital formats that allow for hyperlinks (e.g., Google Docs, Microsoft Word, Adobe Acrobat) can help you more readily differentiate content for students by interest, readiness, and learning profile; students can choose what level of support they want as they learn. A paragraph being read in history class might be linked to a glossary of terms that students can access when needed. A hyperlinked document can facilitate students exploring content more deeply, such as when a student reading an encyclopedia entry on a website clicks on media links or diagrams to expand their knowledge. Annotating key vocabulary and concepts, as well as points to check understanding, provides the additional scaffolding that is helpful to some or even all students.

Match Content with the Most Powerful Medium

As previously mentioned, some of the most challenging content for students surrounds abstract concepts or complex phenomena. Consider for a moment how hard it is to distinguish between a mammal and a reptile, to grasp how the Earth rotates and revolves around the sun, or why it is important to "carry the 1" to the greater unit when adding.

As you consider content differentiation, it is important to match the content being taught with the best mode representing it. And you have a lot of choices, from simulations, animations, and videos to concept maps and diagrams; digital stories, audio recordings, and screencasts; and virtual or augmented reality. For example, when teaching mitosis, a simulation showing how cells divide is a better choice for most students than a 2D concept map illustrating the same ideas. The questions to ask yourself are *What are the best ways to teach this content? With what technologies? And to which students?*

Compared with lectures or text alone, multimedia presentations add value to content instruction. You're able to share more and different information for learners to absorb, consider, and remember. We have also found that video and interactive features used in instruction can make content come alive—feel more "real" and be more interesting to a broader swath of students. "New media" options come with additional affordances, too, including built-in learner control and self-paced engagement. Some formats can be easily reviewed multiple times, or students can stop and start at certain points or rewatch as needed.

Using Digital Tools to Address the 4Es and Respond to Barriers

Incorporating digital tools can greatly influence how well and how often teachers are able to differentiate content for students. The right tools implemented in the right way can address some of the practical challenges teachers often face, such as organization, access to resources, or stretching in too many directions at once. The proper tools help students make good choices and access content in the way that works best for their learning.

When using digital tools to make learning more equitable, efficient, effective, and engaging, consider tools that match content to learners' readiness, present content in a visual snapshot, organize content materials for ready access, enable annotating materials, and help "curate" content.

Analyze the Readability of Text to Match Content to Learner Level

Learning about content is more equitable when there is a match between what students need to learn and the reading level of the content they are expected to review. Teachers are familiar with scales such as Flesch-Kincaid and Lexile. In addition to online tools for identifying the readability level of digital text (e.g., Prepostseo, Readable), the Microsoft Word Spelling and Grammar tool can be used to generate a "readability score." MS Word uses the Flesch-Kincaid scale, which calculates reading-level year and month based on the number of words in each sentence and the number of syllables in each word.

When students also learn to use digital tools to analyze the readability of text, it empowers them to get what they need without having to ask their teachers for help (freeing up teachers to provide other types of support). This skill is essential—and will need to be taught—when giving students the choice and freedom to select their own materials for projects and reports. Students copy an excerpt of the text, check its level, and compare it with their ability to read the text. If it appears to be too hard, then they know to look for a different source that is more appropriate. If there are no appropriate alternatives, or if the students (or you) want to use the source anyway, then other technologies could be employed to simplify or reword the content, so it is clearer to more students. Google Text Simplifier and Rewordify can be used in this way, as can a generative AI tool prompted to explain a complex topic. One constraint of readability tools is that they are difficult for younger learners and some students to use. In such cases, teachers will need to check the readability of text when curating materials for their students—organizing a selection of materials around reading levels.

Represent Content in a Visual Snapshot

For most students, mastering content involves more than simply listening to the material or reading it. This is why multiple representations of content, such as the type offered by word clouds, can be a helpful way to differentiate content.

A **word cloud**, sometimes referred to as a "tag cloud," is a graphic visualization of content information produced using an app or web-based tool. Word clouds are created by pasting a passage of text (e.g., a book chapter, an encyclopedia entry, a news story) into the app, which then analyzes the text to determine the hierarchy of words in relation to one another. Words are then displayed in different font sizes depending on their place in the hierarchy, with those higher up appearing larger. Word cloud apps include features that allow text to be displayed in different fonts and configurations (e.g., shapes, orientation). Providing students with this visualization or snapshot of content gives them a type of alternative access to the main ideas; many students find word clouds a helpful tool for supporting their engagement with content. They are a particularly helpful tool for learners who need to develop literacy skills (e.g., young learners, multilingual learners, learners with low vision; see Miley & Read, 2011).

You can use word clouds to differentiate content in different ways. For example, you might show a word cloud at the beginning of a presentation and ask students to anticipate which ideas they will be exploring and which of these will be the most important. You might show one before beginning discussion of a text or video assigned for homework to stimulate students' memory of the material. Or you might encourage students to create word clouds from the text in each chapter of their digital textbook as an advance organizer before reading or create one using a reflective self-assessment journal to identify major themes in what they've studied. One noteworthy constraint of word clouds is that they should not be used as a substitute for reading a complete passage of text.

Organize Content Materials for Ready Access

When content is organized so that students can access it easily, it streamlines the learning process, saving time and energy. There are many low-tech methods for doing so, but web-based tools offer the affordance that they can be used by many students simultaneously and from different locations (in and outside the classroom). Bookmarking tools (e.g., Diigo, Symbaloo) facilitate the creation of a visually appealing collection of resources for learning support, such as links to the course textbook, the PBS Kids website, Smithsonian Learning Lab, and Merriam-Webster.

Virtual bulletin boards (e.g., IdeaBoardz, Miro, Padlet, Wakelet) also can be helpful for organizing resources for student access. These allow teachers to create a virtual space that can be shared with students using a simple, short URL or a QR code. In the virtual space, teachers can place text, images, multimedia, and more in organized "chunks" or categories to make accessing content materials quick and easy.

Annotate Text and Videos to Customize Materials

Customizing text and video materials promotes greater comprehension among students and leads to more effective learning (Tseng, 2021). One method of adapting content to meet learner needs is annotation, "a note added to a text" (Kalir & Garcia, 2021, p. 12), including video and multimedia presentations. Annotation is a particularly useful strategy when differentiating content based on students' readiness. For instance, you might annotate key academic vocabulary students should know, while also providing additional information that is important to student comprehension. Annotation ranges from using sticky notes to manually marking up text to adding a comment to a word-processed document or video. It can also involve using a social annotation tool or platform (e.g., Annotate, hypothes.is, Perusall).

An affordance of annotating with a web-based tool is that the material can be accessed and marked up collaboratively and simultaneously by several students. One constraint to annotating is that some students find annotations distracting or overwhelming; another is that some students may overwrite other students' annotations. Therefore, it is important to ensure students understand how annotation works and to set ground rules for using the tool.

Curate Content with Playlists

When students have an opportunity to learn in more personalized ways, such as from a collection of materials curated just for them, it often results in more engaged learning (Zheng et al., 2022). *Playlists* (sometimes referred to as "mixtapes") are curated digital content designed for individual or small groups of students. A playlist can be thought of as an "individual digital assignment chart" (Gonzalez, 2016, para. 2) that allows students to work through a lesson or assignment at their own pace and incorporates resources tailored to each student's needs.

Playlists can include a variety of activities and instructions: links to videos, online articles, or interactive lessons; and reading assignments from texts or written exercises from a station or center in the classroom. A playlist might have space for students to add notes and check off when they've completed a segment; you can also embed checkpoints to monitor student progress.

Questions for Reflection

- Reflect on the content you differentiate in your teaching. What are some benefits for incorporating technology-mediated content to differentiate instruction?
- How often do you use multimedia presentations, visual snapshots like word clouds, or annotation tools to support student access to content?
- How does the technology you use address the 4Es and support differentiated instruction?

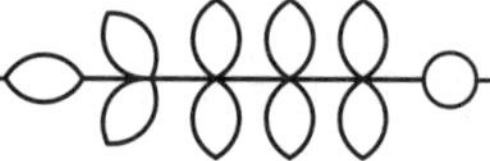

7

Differentiating the Learning Process

This chapter covers...

- The various components of the learning process.
- Micro-differentiation versus macro-differentiation.
- The key practices that support successful learning process differentiation.
- How to use digital tools to reduce barriers and address the 4Es when differentiating the learning process.

Imagine a class of 3rd graders on their way to the school cafeteria. Picture that wriggling line of small humans moving together along a hallway—some hopping or skipping, others swaggering, and one rolling in a wheelchair. Under their teacher's watchful guidance, each student demonstrates their own, singular way of moving toward their destination.

This image is a powerful one for conceptualizing the learning process in a differentiated classroom. Here, all learners share a common destination—the mastery of academic standards—but, with the assistance of their teacher, they can arrive at it in their own distinct way.

What Is the Learning Process?

The term *learning process* refers to any instructional experience that engages students in the practices required to develop new skills and make sense of new knowledge. Through a teacher's implementation of plans for the learning process, students are provided with the stimulation (i.e., emotional, sensory, intellectual, physical) required to acquire, retain, and apply new competencies and understandings, which might also be referred to as *goals, objectives,* or *KUDs.* The learning process is a success when students have appropriated the content being studied and made it their own.

Various aspects of the learning context, or *learning setting,* influence a teacher's choice of the activities, materials, and tools to use during the learning process. Everything—the academic level, the subject area, the details of the physical environment, learner characteristics, the specific learning goals—factors into the design of the learning process. Thus, the learning process itself is highly variable.

The goal for the learning process, both in a differentiated setting and in a standard one, is to support students as they master, appropriate, and apply new learning. What is different in a well-run differentiated classroom is that **decisions about the learning process are governed by what will best help all students learn** rather than other factors, including the teacher's professional habits. Teachers who differentiate effectively do so by building learning experiences to be as effective as possible for the individual students in their classroom. They factor in the possible activities and structures, as well as the materials and tools necessary to make each student's learning experience a successful one. These teachers appreciate that some choices might create experiences that are easier for some students than others—and they plan to mitigate this in multiple ways—by routinely building in methods that are universally supportive of students with different learning needs. For example, they might routinely offer instructions in more than one format (e.g., verbal, written, visual). They also map out how they will adapt activities for different learners (e.g., have both graphic organizers and glossaries at the ready). They anticipate where difficulties might occur and offer materials that provide just-in-time support when needed. Thanks to their thoughtful learning design, procedures are in place so that *when* (not *if*) students need support, they know how to get it without disrupting the flow of the class.

Teachers adept at differentiation adjust these processes in response to what they know about their students, which is why they are continually trying to learn as much as they can about students through assessment (see

Chapters 4 and 5) and regularly engage students in activities that prompt them to reflect on and learn from their performance. Over time, with effort, and across circumstances, these teachers become expert decision makers whose choices enhance their students' interest and engagement in the learning process. Their work also reduces the confusion, frustration, and unproductive struggles students can experience when they are striving to meet the goals for their learning but lack the necessary supports.

All aspects of the learning process—from experiences or activities to materials and tools and the variety and level of human support provided by others—contribute to a student's involvement with the content being learned and the quality of their participation in sense-making and appropriation activities.

Experiences, Activities, and Materials

Experiences and activities are means through which students engage with what they are learning, whether that's participation in a particular instructional approach (e.g., guided inquiry), completion of a set of tasks (e.g., following a checklist of experimentation procedures), or using certain skills (e.g., shooting a foul shot, creating an outline). The **materials** involved in the learning process help students complete the unit's (or lesson's) expected activities and achieve its goals. These might include textbooks and other reading material, video and audio recordings, as well as any instructions or resources that aid task engagement and completion. Worksheets that provide guided practice, diagrams on a whiteboard, reading prediction guides, graphic organizers, and checklists are all useful materials in the learning process. A good proportion of supportive and scaffolding materials is developed by the teachers themselves.

Tools

When students are asked to participate in learning activities, they often need to use tools, ranging from simple items (e.g., ruler, egg carton, scissors) to more complicated ones (e.g., microscope, tablet, clicker, website). Different tools support the learning process in a variety of different ways.

In a differentiated classroom, tool use is flexible. Often, the same tool is available to all learners as a matter of course; for example, all students might use a protractor when learning how to measure angles. At other times, different tools are used by individual learners to provide appropriate levels of challenge. For example, a teacher might ask some students to use a calculator and others to use a spreadsheet to calculate their average grade for the term. When it comes to tool assignment, various factors motivate the teacher's decision: student comfort with different tools, the amount of support students need or receive from a tool, or the availability of the tools.

Human Support

Other people can assist in the learning process, providing both social support and just-in-time interventions that assist a student's success. In a differentiated classroom, teachers plan proactively to provide support to learners rather than responding "on the fly" to needs as they emerge. One way of providing support is through interactions with others. Sometimes the "other" is the teacher (who might work with individuals or groups); sometimes the other might be a peer, a classroom aide or specialist teacher, or a subject-area expert (e.g., scientist, artist, author).

Approaches to Differentiating the Learning Process

Recognizing what can be differentiated in the learning process is the first step toward making learning work better for all students in the classroom. Deciding how this differentiation is best achieved comes next and is easier to achieve—with the right guidance and mindset.

Sometimes the design for a learning process is not differentiated, in which cases, teachers can make add-on modifications. Other times, the design for the learning process contains built-in support for differentiation. Both methods of differentiation address the activities, tools, resources, and human support for learning and effectively respond to variability in students' interests, readiness, and learning profile. Teachers who differentiate instruction routinely use a combination of the two approaches.

Micro-differentiation

Micro-differentiation of the learning process is when you plan for options or adjustments that can make learning work better for students (in addition to the general learning process being implemented). Micro-differentiation addresses variability in student interest, readiness, and learning profile. A hands-on activity, such as one that asks students to gain knowledge through the manipulation of objects, is not intentionally differentiated in its design. However, this same learning experience can be differentiated if you allow students to work together as partners or in groups and provide varying levels of explanation in written and oral instructions.

Incorporating micro-differentiation strategies allows a teacher to adjust the learning process for **interest**, by encouraging students to practice new language arts skills by writing about topics of personal interest; for **learning profile**, by giving students the option of working alone or with a peer; and for **readiness**, by encouraging students to incorporate tools (e.g., a formula sheet, calculator) that free them to focus on content application. Some teachers incorporate student interests into a sense-making activity (e.g., compare this new concept to your favorite hobby) or differentiate for readiness by grouping students who work at the same speed.

Micro-differentiation requires little change to the design for a learning process. Instead, you adjust the amount of time allotted for a task, provide checklists or instructions in more than one format (e.g., text, audio, video), or encourage students to use graphic organizers or digital tools as needed. You can also create different discussion or reflection prompts for students based on their level of familiarity with and mastery of content or modify how often you interact with students. Basically, micro-differentiation entails considering students' access and engagement with the content, given their readiness, learning profiles, and interests, and figuring out the various types of support they need.

Here are some additional examples of micro-differentiation strategies:

- **Differentiate opportunities for students to make sense of or "process" the material being studied.** What sorts of physical, cognitive, emotional, and social stimuli can you provide to grab students' attention or tap into their interests? How can you build in opportunities to make content more relevant, inviting, or reflective of your students? Is there a way to offer students choice in sense-making activities? Can you vary the modes of expression and the supports (e.g., Venn diagrams, fishbone charts) available to students?

- **Differentiate the materials available to students.** Can you offer real-world examples and other resources as opposed to or in addition to textbooks? If you're giving students access to electronic resources, does it make sense to curate a selection for students to choose from? What are the affordances and constraints of digital resources? Are they able to be equitably used by all?
- **Differentiate the tools available to students based on readiness or learning profile.** Will low-tech tools remove distraction for some students? Are there digital tools that could make the learning process more engaging for students, reduce tedium, remove barriers, or reduce unproductive struggle?
- **Differentiate the human supports offered for learning.** Does it make sense to use heterogeneous or homogenous grouping? Peer teaching or other student interactions? Do you need to prepare guided notes, annotated material, or just-in-time recorded instructions or teachings that students can access? Are there other people (e.g., experts, aides, in-person and virtual volunteers) who could also support students?

Macro-differentiation

With macro-differentiation, the design for the learning process involves a structured model or strategy that contains built-in support for differentiation within its different stages or steps. Incorporating macro-differentiation models requires effort, time, and professional expertise but offers substantial benefits for students.

In macro-differentiation lessons are deliberately designed to ensure flexibility, choice, and the strategic use of grouping. They are more complex in structure and often incorporate specialized materials or tools (e.g., learning organizers, hyperlinked instructions, web pages, and playlists) as well as defined roles for students and teachers.

Tiered assignments, for example, present expectations for students' attainment of content standards at different levels and with varying degrees of support from the assignments' built-in scaffolds and from the teacher. Learning contracts, another example of macro-differentiation, typically involve the teacher partnering with each individual student to develop a negotiated set of learning goals based on the content standards. In a high school economics class, students might learn about inflation and its primary effect (i.e., rising costs for goods and services) and the ways it influences individuals and various aspects of the economy. The teacher might ask students to generate personal lists of what they can do to attain these goals. Some students might formulate a list of activities that require them to consult existing resources (e.g., books and articles posted online) in order to write a report expanding and refining their knowledge of inflation. Other students might begin by exploring these resources and summarize their findings in another manner (e.g., a diagram with annotations), but then do independent research to develop additional skills, as well as conduct interviews with several people they know about how inflation affects them. They might use their research to prepare "case studies" to share with their classmates and generate questions for further study. With learning contracts, students have a lot of freedom to choose what is needed for their success, and the act of designing the contracts is itself a complex and rigorous learning task that teachers must be prepared to scaffold.

Macro-differentiation accounts for the intricacies of the different types of experiences students take part in during the learning process. There are many different macro-differentiation models, including some discussed in the remainder of this chapter.

Support for the Learning Experience

Tomlinson (2017a) describes a variety of methods for providing support during the learning process; her "differentiation equalizer" (see Figure 7.1) is a visual tool that is useful when considering the ways that curriculum content differs and the ways that the learning process might be adjusted in response.

The equalizer and its associated thinking supports both micro- and macro-differentiation. It prompts educational designers to consider the ways that the content in a learning experience might vary and ways to provide support for that learning experience. For example, to support students learning an abstract concept like measurement, you might provide concrete experiences (e.g., measuring with rulers or scales). To support the completion of a complex task, you could provide procedural lists that deconstruct the task into simpler "chunks."

Key Practices for Differentiating the Learning Process

Although there are many ways to differentiate the learning process, there are a few key practices that belong in every educational designer's skill set: (1) matching the learning process to the development of different types of knowledge, (2) incorporating choice, and (3) implementing strategies with defined and powerful structures.

Match the Learning Process to the Type of Knowledge

The revised Bloom's taxonomy (Anderson et al., 2001) outlines four categories of knowledge students are typically expected to master:

- **Factual knowledge**—the basic and essential elements a person must know;
- **Procedural knowledge**—how to do something and when it is appropriate to do it;
- **Conceptional knowledge**—the relationship between classifications and categories; and
- **Metacognitive knowledge**—understanding cognitive tasks and one's own thinking and learning.

A well-constructed learning process promotes students' mastery of these knowledge types as well as the attainment of other social, emotional, and physical goals. It does this by activating a variety of cognitive processes, including remembering, understanding, applying, analyzing, evaluating, and creating. A differentiated learning process includes the experiences necessary for each student to make sense of the content and appropriate it. For example, a social studies teacher exposes students to the concepts of *needs and wants* (the content) in a slide presentation. Then the teacher asks them to remember and discuss these concepts with their peers (the

FIGURE 7.1
The Differentiated Instruction "Equalizer"

Dimension	Low end	High end
1. Information, Ideas, Materials, Applications	Foundational	Transformational
2. Representations, Ideas, Applications, Materials	Concrete	Abstract
3. Resources, Research, Issues, Problems, Skills, Goals	Simple	Complex
4. Disciplinary Connections, Directions, Stages of Development	Single Facet	Multiple Facets
5. Application, Insight, Transfer	Small Leap	Great Leap
6. Solutions, Decisions, Approaches	More Structured	More Open
7. In Process, in Research, in Products	Clearly Defined Problems	Fuzzy Problems
8. Planning, Designing, Monitoring	Dependent	More Independent
9. Pace of Study, Pace of Thought	Slower	Quicker

Source: Adapted from *The Differentiated Classroom* (2nd ed.), by C. A. Tomlinson, 2014, p. 186.
Copyright © 2014 ASCD.

learning process). The content and the process work together like a pair of legs, moving students toward the goals of learning.

Certain instructional approaches are better suited to the acquisition and mastery of particular types of knowledge (Kilbane & Milman, 2014). For example, if students are expected to "bank" or memorize **factual knowledge**, such as the names and components of different body systems, flash cards and instructional games are appropriate approaches. If students need to master **procedural knowledge**, such as how to complete a geometric proof, the Direct Instruction Model (Kilbane & Milman, 2014) would be a good fit, because it provides the lesson's objectives, an introduction to new content, guided practice, and independent practice. Students who need to learn **conceptual knowledge** might be helped using Taba's Inductive Model (Taba et al., 1971). Responding through writing or speaking to reflective prompts is a powerful way of supporting students' **metacognitive knowledge**. Speaking of metacognition, after selecting an approach that suits the instructional purpose, and as they guide students through that process, the most effective teachers call attention to how learning methods function as specialized tools that work best when properly matched with compatible tasks.

Incorporate Choice

When you differentiate instruction, in addition to teaching students academic content, you are also facilitating their development as independent learners. Students benefit from opportunities to exercise autonomy and agency as they make choices that affect their learning (Marshall, 2022; Merrill & Gonser, 2021; Milman & Vanden Boogart, 2024). Although choice is an important ingredient for differentiating all aspects of learning, it is crucial in the learning process where there are many potential opportunities to incorporate student choice.

Be aware that too much choice can be overwhelming for some students, and it can divert focus from the goals for the learning process. When providing choices, present them in an organized and clear manner so students can benefit from the range of options without suffering unnecessary confusion or distraction. Operational technologies and digital tools can be helpful, for example, in presenting the steps of the learning process numerically and including hyperlinks to options for pedagogical tools (e.g., apps, online tools) and materials (e.g., graphic organizers, websites) in each step. Learning management systems (e.g., Blackboard, Canvas) can also support the presentation of different materials and means by which students navigate the learning process. Again, it is important that choices are clear and presented in a manner that minimizes students' cognitive load. The focus should be on doing the work of learning, not on trying to understand the many options they may choose from for support.

Effective teachers go beyond simply offering a choice; they work to stimulate as much learning as possible and challenge students to learn from their choices. Whether asking students directly or having them write a reflection or engage in self-assessment, you should encourage them to judge the efficacy and effect of their choice. What choice did they make? What were their reasons for this choice? What happened as a result of this choice? How did it affect their learning? Was it a "good" choice? Would they make the same choice again? What did they learn from their choice that will affect their future actions or thinking?

Choice can be integrated using macro-differentiation strategies such as choice boards, strategies like RAFTs, interest centers and interest groups, and tiered instruction.

Choice boards (e.g., bingo boards, lists, menus, columns) present students with a selection of activities, structuring how they will engage with the content. The choices you offer can vary by interest, depth, and breadth. For example, in a 2nd grade classroom where a teacher is differentiating for interest, students might be presented with three options (e.g., flamingos, pelicans, cardinals) for making sense of the concept of a bird, another three options (e.g., parrots, tundra swans, bluebirds) when learning about bird habitats, and three more (e.g., piping plovers, peregrine falcons, and mallards) for learning about bird habits. Students also choose the learning activities they will undertake from two or more options.

With digital choice boards, you hyperlink the students' options to a collection of content materials; students also select a way to document and process what they are learning (e.g., taking notes, filling in a worksheet, making an audio recording on an mp3 player). The various hyperlinks provide progressively more detailed information—related assignment steps, rubrics, and examples. The digital presentation of information and materials helps overcome some of the organizational challenges associated with choice. Although they typically take a bit more effort and time at the front end when developing, having choice boards in digital format makes them easy to edit; less work will be required to make tweaks the following school year or for use with a different group of students.

RAFT (i.e., role, audience, format, topic) is a macro-differentiation strategy that incorporates choice in the learning process, encourages creativity, and promotes writing across content areas (see Martlett, n.d.). Students exercise choice over different RAFT components—the role they take, the audience they're communicating to, the format the expression takes, and the topic they write about. For example, in a library/media class, students might apply what they have learned about plagiarism (the topic) by responding to a set of guidelines (e.g., what it is, why it is wrong, what constitutes it, examples); they choose the format of their response (e.g., a skit, a news article, a memo), their role (e.g., an author, a book, a publisher), and their audience (e.g., aspiring authors). With the RAFT model, you can limit or expand the number of choices you offer.

Using technology tools can enhance RAFT assignments; with online platforms (e.g., Google Docs, Padlet), students can collaborate, share, and comment on each one another's work. Members of the extended learning community (see Chapter 3) can also be invited to engage with multimedia discussion tools (e.g., VoiceThread). Products for RAFT assignments can range from jingles, commercials, or advertisements to cartoons; op-ed pieces, essays, letters, or monologues; skits; and news stories. Using digital tools (e.g., Canva, Powtoon, Storybird), students can create multimedia products (e.g., posters, stories, videos).

Interest centers (typically used with younger students) and **interest groups** (more commonly used with older students) offer activities designed and organized around specific learner interests. The teacher develops a list of topics students have expressed interest in (focusing on content standards) and then designs activities that are appropriate to both the learners and the topic. Students' interests serve as great motivators in learning; using different operational and pedagogical technologies (e.g., displaying options on a digital whiteboard, a web page displayed on a tablet or computer) acts as an additional motivator. Digital tools can help learners quickly locate information related to their interests or be used in learning centers to encourage student accountability.

Implement Strategies with Powerful Structures and Built-in Support

Not all strategies are created equal. Some strategies are powerful because they build in options for choice. Other strategies have carefully defined structures that build in sense-making activities and accommodate students getting support "just in time" as needed.

Tiered instruction is a macro-differentiation strategy that involves engaging students with the content being studied at intentionally varied levels of difficulty. Students engage with the same learning objectives but the degrees of complexity, structure, number of steps, or level of independence are varied. For instance, all students in a 5th grade class are learning about rounding decimals, but the level of challenge differs. One group might be required (or might choose) to round up to the hundreds place; other students might round to the thousandths, depending on their background with adding, subtracting, multiplying, and dividing fractions. The differentiation equalizer (see Figure 7.1) is a helpful tool when considering variations in tiering.

When planning a tiered learning process, create one version of the learning process and then develop additional versions at other levels. Tiered instruction builds on Vygotsky's (1978) zone of proximal development (ZPD), the learning conditions or "space" where students experience the right amount of challenge and support for their optimal growth. A cornerstone of differentiated classrooms is varying levels of difficulty to address learning goals or objectives—to do so successfully requires designing instruction with students' ZPD in mind.

HyperDocs (see hyperdocs.co) are digital lesson structures designed to offer support for content differentiation. HyperDocs incorporate technology to build on the powerful 5E Model (initially Atkin & Karplus, 1962, then Bybee & Landes, 1990). The accommodating digital format offers a lot of flexibility and can readily incorporate assistive tools or web browser extensions that customize the text for processing via different sensory modalities (e.g., touch, listening). Additionally, the ability to integrate hyperlinks opens up possibilities for extending learning support throughout the learning process.

The six steps in the HyperDocs structure (including three from the 5E model) are as follows:

1. **Engage.** This is some type of "hook" to engage learners in the topic. For instance, students learning about the American Revolution might start by listening to songs or looking at art depicting this period. Multimedia animations or short video clips might be included in this part of the HyperDoc to add further details and promote deeper engagement.
2. **Explore.** In this stage, students actively explore content about the topic. For instance, students might read or watch content to understand why and how the American Revolution happened. Linked materials and websites that are embedded within the text could direct students through various steps or activities that they encounter only when they need help or to stay focused on their exploration and learning.
3. **Explain.** This portion of the lesson incorporates direct instruction (e.g., lecture) to explain the content. In our example, the teacher shows students a timeline and synopsis of major events and people involved in the American Revolution and the class discusses it, reflecting on what they have explored. A teacher's demonstration might be recorded and linked to the HyperDoc to accommodate students progressing through the learning at different paces, students who would benefit from repeated exposure to the demonstration, and students who need to catch up after an absence.
4. **Apply.** For this portion of the lesson, teachers create an activity that applies the content being learned to develop deeper understanding. Students might be asked to create a news article that reports on what they have learned about the American Revolution along with a town crier's short summary to publicize it.
5. **Reflect and share.** This is where teachers ask students to reflect on and share their understanding through any number of modes. For example, students might be asked to informally think-pair-share in

small groups or complete a formal, rubric-guided self-assessment to examine how well they followed directions or employed various types of thinking skills.

6. **Extend.** In this last part of Hyperdocs, teachers provide more opportunities to learn the content. This is useful for students who wish to delve deeper into the subject matter, as well as for those who might complete their required work earlier than others. Here, students might have an opportunity to connect with an expert via videoconferencing or review materials available through historical archives that "real-world" professionals use.

The step-by-step structure of **WebQuests** (Dodge, 1997) similarly ensures powerful learning experiences (e.g., promoting thinking skills, real-world applications, opportunities to work with peers) and builds in support for student learning. WebQuests promote more efficient use of web-based resources for academic learning and more effective and engaging learning for students through incorporation of curated content resources and learning supports. All WebQuests follow the same structure:

1. An **introduction** that sets the stage, generates student interest, and provides some background information;
2. A **task** that is age-appropriate, focused on curriculum standards, within students' ZPD, interesting, and linked to real-world applications;
3. A curated set of **information sources** required to complete the task;
4. A description of the **process** in discrete, manageable steps that learners will execute to complete the task;
5. **Guidance** and other supports to assist students in organizing and analyzing the information they acquire (e.g., guiding questions, categories, timelines, maps); and
6. A **conclusion** that wraps up the quest and captures what has been learned.

The WebQuest model has other distinguishing characteristics designed to reflect ideas from theory (e.g., ideas about motivation and engagement), research (e.g., the importance of social dimensions of learning), and educational "best practice" (e.g., organization, predictable structure, close proximity of resources to instructions).

WebQuests are a great tool for differentiating instruction. You can create your own using cloud-based documents with hyperlinks and webpages, or specialized tools (e.g., QuestGarden) to suit your setting and grade level.

Using Digital Tools to Address the 4Es and Respond to Barriers

The challenges involved in implementing a differentiated learning process sometimes keep teachers from engaging in this practice as effectively and as frequently as they would like. Teachers are painfully aware that offering multiple pathways through a learning experience can distract or confuse some students; offering choices can overwhelm others, and giving the option for working in groups can produce noise levels that make thinking difficult for everyone. With this type of design for learning, it's also necessary to incorporate ways to keep track of student progress and to identify when students need extra support.

Having the right tool set can help you address these barriers while also making learning more equitable, efficient, effective, and engaging. Differentiating the learning process is more successful with digital tools that (1) expedite student access to instructions and materials, (2) facilitate collaboration, and (3) track progress.

Expedite Access to Instructions and Materials

QR codes ("quick response" codes) are a regular fixture of contemporary life—in restaurants (in lieu of a paper menu), in stores (to offer additional information about merchandise or coupons), and at sporting or entertainment events (e.g., ticketing, links to program guides). In a differentiated classroom, these two-dimensional bar codes can make it easier to navigate differentiated learning processes, among other educational uses.

QR codes can be created and read using a QR code generator, a QR code reader, and mobile devices with a camera (e.g., smartphone, iPad). They can also be created online using web-based tools (e.g., Delivr, Kaywa QR code), or with apps (e.g., QRCode Monkey, smartphone shortcut). QR codes linked to resources help guide students through the steps of the learning process. You might link to learning process guidelines (e.g., rubrics, standards), instructions (e.g., directions, steps, frequently asked questions), resources (e.g., websites, videos, tutorials), or documents (e.g., checklists, help documents, examples). QR codes instantly connect learners to what they need to complete a task, report on their progress, or move their learning forward. One affordance of using QR codes is that they are easy for young learners and generally make content more accessible. Scanning a code is much simpler than remembering or looking up and then typing in a code.

Facilitate Collaboration

Sometimes the noise levels in a classroom rise to high levels when students are engaged in a meaningful learning experience. Sharing ideas, resources, and working together, if not controlled, can be inequitable, negatively affecting some students (e.g., those with sensory or attention challenges).

Social learning doesn't have to be noisy. In a virtual learning environment, breakout rooms are an additional and appealing option. In the physical classroom, you can encourage students to use chat tools (e.g., Google Chat, Backchannel Chat) or virtual bulletin boards (e.g., IdeaBoardz, Padlet, Wakelet) to interact around ideas and share resources without speaking aloud. With virtual bulletin boards, students log in to a shared virtual space and post messages on "sticky notes" or upload resources (e.g., images, links, sound/video files) to help with the learning process. These tools offer additional advantages in that a record of interactions and collaborations is logged, which can be reviewed by the group or the teacher to understand the nature and depth of their exchanges.

Track Progress

One of the most challenging aspects of differentiated learning processes is that their complexity can make it harder to monitor and log student progress toward meeting goals and objectives. Digital tools can break down this barrier to successful learning. One of the simplest ways to track student progress is to use a cloud-based tool—a shared spreadsheet, document, or form. The teacher logs the various steps in the learning process, with checkpoints where students should report on their activities. This puts students in charge of their own auditing and builds their independence. It shifts responsibility from the teacher, who then must only ensure students are reporting and progressing through the learning process.

Keeping track of students' progress includes collecting and organizing the different kinds of information to be shared. Whether you use a shared spreadsheet or a learning management system (e.g., Canvas, PowerSchool), you'll need to plan for collecting information. You might have students, or groups of students, indicate progress toward the completion of distinct tasks in the learning process using a binary "yes/no" option or indicate a percentage of total completion (e.g., scale of 1–5; estimate/indicator of 10%, 20%, 30%).

It can also be helpful to allow students to communicate their degree of independence or success whenever they are working to complete a task or seeking help from the teacher. A popular means of doing this is to have students register a green mark ("Doing fine!"), yellow mark ("Could use some help, please!"), or a red mark ("Whoa! HELP ME!"). Leaving a space in the progress tracking tool where students can log comments is also helpful. This type of input allows you to quickly identify whether and where oversight might be needed, so that you can better understand how students are progressing with different aspects of their learning. It will help you balance students' developing independence with opportunities for intervention when that is what's needed.

Questions for Reflection

- What are some ways that you currently differentiate the learning process? What else might you do in the future?
- Do your lesson plans incorporate some of the strategies for differentiating the process of instruction mentioned in this chapter? If not, where might you integrate them?
- How might you also integrate technology while differentiating the process of instruction?
- Are there any specific learning designs offering specialized support for students as they process ideas and work to apply new skills that you can incorporate to remove obstacles to student learning?
- Are there effective micro-differentiations that you can incorporate to add an additional layer of support for students as they engage with the macro-differentiation strategy being used?

8

Differentiating Learning Products

This chapter covers…

- The nature of a "learning product."
- The best way to approach designing and differentiating learning products.
- The key practices that will help students produce valuable and enriching learning products.
- How to use digital tools to reduce barriers and address the 4Es when differentiating learning products.

The impulse to create is a fundamental human drive—one that a teacher in a differentiated classroom can capitalize on to deepen student learning. Creating a learning product gives students an opportunity to express the knowledge and skills they have acquired. The output—whether it's a podcast, a pamphlet, a model, a traditional written or oral report, or any other product—is a means for both self-expression and summative assessment. Often, differentiating learning products requires that you also differentiate the content (see Chapter 6) and process (see Chapter 7).

What Is a Learning Product?

The term *learning product,* or just *product,* refers to the output that students develop at the request of their teacher following a significant period of learning (e.g., a unit, term, or marking period). Product assignments give students creative ways to express themselves and what they have learned. The best ones challenge students to apply the knowledge and skills they are developing through creation or performance, using various tools and materials. For example, a student asked to construct a diorama of a wetland habitat operationalizes what they have learned about the interdependence of organisms in a physical format. The teacher is able to appraise their learning by considering how well the diorama demonstrates an understanding of the ecosystem's different components and their healthy balance.

The applied and real-world nature of products tends to make them feel meaningful and rewarding. Students at all grade levels generally approach product-creation assignments with increased enthusiasm, excitement, and motivation.

Learning products complement more traditional summative assessment measures such as tests, quizzes, compositions, and lab reports, offering more flexibility in terms of student choice and self-expression. Thus, they are especially valuable in the differentiated classroom, where teachers strive to promote student ownership of learning and value students' expression of their aptitudes, talents, and unique accomplishments. Teachers who differentiate effectively give product assignments frequently and intentionally. They design these assignments carefully to include built-in support options that minimize confusion, aid completion, and give students various ways to showcase their learning and personal aptitudes.

As is the case with other assessment methods, a high-quality product yields in-depth and accurate information about a student's progress toward mastering standards and objectives. It also addresses or eliminates any barriers with the potential to obscure what a student is really and truly capable of doing. Understanding how to design high-quality product assignments is a specialized competency that all teachers should cultivate.

Although all learning products communicate important information about the students who create them, product assignments vary considerably from one another. The standards they address, method used to present them, number of steps involved, complexity of these steps, degree of teacher guidance, and whether they involve collaboration with peers are unique from assignment to assignment.

Products also vary in format and the related modes of expression they involve. The range of possibilities is nearly endless. Products might tap into students' **artistic abilities** (e.g., design a pamphlet, draw a cartoon, make a map, develop a logo, construct a model); their **musical talents** (e.g., write a song, choreograph a dance); their **ability to distill or collect** (e.g., create a museum, fill a bag with artifacts, develop a glossary, annotate content); their **technological knowledge** (e.g., create a website, design a virtual tour, create a video or multimedia presentation, design a simulation); their **writing abilities** (e.g., create a newspaper or magazine, write a legend or other fictional piece), or some combination of these talents—and others!

Designing and Differentiating Learning Products

In the differentiated classroom, learning products are a powerful means of adjusting learning in response to students' readiness, interest, and learning profile. Incorporating products in a way that effectively promotes student learning is a process that includes (1) focusing clearly on specified standards, (2) considering the affordances and constraints of different formats and tools, and (3) identifying the "fit" between learners and product formats and tools.

Focus on Specified Standards

To design a learning product assignment, you need to identify the knowledge and skills students are responsible for learning, determine which aspects to incorporate in the product, and plan the instructional activities that will lead to its creation. Any significant period of learning addresses numerous and varied learning standards, and it is impossible to integrate them all in the creation of a single learning product. You want to focus on something that's both comprehensible and manageable for students. Tomlinson (2017a) advises asking yourself these questions:

- What understandings do you want students to further refine as they develop the product?
- What personal dispositions (e.g., attention to detail, perseverance, strategic choices, collaboration) might they cultivate?
- What technical skills, if any, do you want them to demonstrate?

It can be helpful to generate a list of the skills and knowledge students are cultivating and then consider which ones are the **most important** to incorporate in the product: those that are most central to what is being learned (particularly crucial for future learning) or of great meaning to students. You also need to identify the skills and knowledge that are **most appropriate** to include in the product: those that are well suited to practical application or to the format the product will take. In this analysis, you may discover that some of the content students are learning is best evaluated using traditional assessment measures or may have already been measured adequately through other means.

Consider Affordances and Constraints of Formats and Tools

What is simultaneously delightful and daunting about designing learning product assignments is that there are so many formats and tools to choose from. These options have great power to promote creativity (Milman & Vanden Boogart, 2024), but guard against elevating entertainment value or aesthetics above substance. When it comes to product assignment design formats, think carefully about the affordances and constraints (see Chapter 2) associated with each and ask the following questions:

- What outputs will allow students to meet the goals for the product? What formats are there to choose from? Which are best for this assignment?
- Given the goals for the product (and the process involved in developing it), what criteria will be important to evaluate as it relates to the content (reflecting curriculum standards) that should be reflected in the product? Are these the same for various format options?
- Are there high- and low-tech tools students might use? What are they? Would offering students a choice of tools be helpful?
- How does it promote or hinder creativity? What can teachers do to educate students about form over substance?
- If digital tools are being used, do they make students' expression of learning more equitable? How do they also make learning more efficient, effective, and engaging?

This kind of reflection will help you better identify formats that might extend students' learning and you select formats that best display students' mastery of knowledge or skills.

For example, creating an infographic using tools like Adobe Express, Canva, or Venngage offers some affordances for demonstrating the life cycle of a monarch butterfly. The step-by-step process provides numerous opportunities for students to examine what they have learned and challenges them to deepen their understanding. The visual format lends itself well to communicating the various developmental stages in the butterfly's life. The shape and color options available in web- or app-based infographic tools make it easy for students to distinguish these development stages from one another and demonstrate the progression. The ability to incorporate blocks of text and spell-check automatically supports their capacity to describe milestone events in the insect's lifespan. Yet, an infographic has some constraints, including that it makes it more difficult to show transitions between stages effectively. Another format (e.g., multimedia presentation) could enable the inclusion of video footage demonstrating how a butterfly emerges from its chrysalis when transitioning between stages.

Identify the Fit Between Learners and Product Formats

The best learning products are a good "fit," responding to the needs of each learner. This means that products are flexible enough to support the expression of all students' knowledge and skills—not just the knowledge or skills of those who happen to find a particular learning product aligns with their specific strengths. This is another occasion where your understanding of your students—their backgrounds, aptitudes, preferences, and predispositions—makes a difference. When selecting product formats, consider these questions:

- How will *all* students be able to demonstrate success given the options for product formats and tools?
- Is it possible to offer students a choice between different formats? If so, what would they need to know or be asked to think about to guide their decisions?
- How would you go about determining the best tools for various product assignments? What role might pre-assessment, formative assessment, and summative assessment play in these decisions over time?

A written product such as a story might be an effective way for students to convey their understanding of the scientific method if they are skilled writers and comfortable using Microsoft Word or Google Docs. However, struggling writers with limited keyboarding skills will have more difficulty communicating their understanding when compared to effective writers and fast keyboarders. Similarly, asking students to create a newspaper using a digital tool such as Canva or Flipsnack (a tool for creating flipbooks) might be a great way for students to express understanding of the Great Depression, but it could present a problem for learners who do not have access to or facility with the selected digital tools. In such cases, you might also give students the option of writing or creating content by hand or teach them how to use the technology tool. If all learning products need to be submitted digitally (e.g., as part of a portfolio; see Chapter 5), students can take a digital photo of their finished work and upload it to the learning management system (with your help or that of a peer). Recognizing how the different factors involved in a product will influence students enables you to design plans for incorporating products more powerfully.

Key Practices for Differentiating Learning Products

Teachers who differentiate products to meet the needs of their students benefit from knowing and having several key practices in their skill set. These include (1) ensuring the products will serve as an effective means of evaluation, (2) using examples and rubrics effectively, (3) ensuring products are culturally responsive, (4) incorporating student voice and choice, and (5) making sure the products are authentic.

Design Products to Promote Effective Evaluation

One challenge associated with any assessment (see Chapters 4 and 5) is that it must capture and outwardly communicate students' internal knowledge and skills. Effective assessments present a clear "signal" about student learning and filter out as much "noise" as possible. For example, an effective written test should communicate how well students understand and retain the content that has been studied (the signal), not how well they understood the directions (the noise).

More complex forms of assessment, including products, have more sources of noise and can obscure what a student knows or can do. Factors related to a product that can generate or alleviate noise include the following:

- **Instructions.** Instructions specify the steps or procedures students should follow when creating their product. How they are presented has a significant effect on how well students understand what is being asked of them—and whether they will succeed in delivering it. If instructions are overlong, too detailed, or do not allow students to interact with the ideas (e.g., checklist), this can create noise and impede student understanding of the assignment. Using numbered lists or checklists helps to ensure students grasp exactly what they need to do.
- **Supports.** Because students will vary in their readiness to complete different kinds of product assignments independently, always make a plan for providing both the human and built-in supports that will eliminate barriers to engagement and completion. Annotation or optional, supplemental video instruction can help. Embedding important nuggets of instruction (e.g., "Stop and discuss your plan with a peer"), links to explainer videos, and definitions of key academic vocabulary can also support students' success with this kind of learning experience.
- **Examples and rubrics.** Although helpful to all students, positive examples and rubrics are even more important for students who need additional support to understand what they are being asked to communicate through their product. Examples of completed products with accompanying rubrics provide a more concrete illustration of expectations and are useful in some cases.
- **Tools.** Tools can range from simple and low-tech (e.g., pencils, paper, crayons, markers) to complex or high-tech (e.g., multimedia tools, digital video editing programs). Digital tools can often expedite tedious processes (e.g., making revision easier) and aid student expression (e.g., when documents come stocked with clip art). However, tools also present a degree of noise that can affect learning as well as its expression and evaluation—when they are a distraction

(allowing students to waste time or misplace energy), when students do not have the support and knowledge to use tools productively, or the technology provides the wrong output (such as when spellcheck fails to catch a grammatical or spelling error or a generative AI tool like ChatGPT provides incorrect information).

Your **instructions** should clearly identify the steps or processes involved; the overall format options for the project and the tools and materials for each step; and resources for students (human or digital) if they need help or assistance during the process of developing the product. Present instructions in "chunks" (e.g., steps), using words, phrases, and diagrams, with an appropriate level of detail. You may need to provide different levels of detail for your learners. For example, a student who intuitively understands school and teacher requests could use a general outline of steps, whereas other students may need detailed descriptions for each step. Consider presenting instructions in multiple formats or languages and formatting text (e.g., bold headings for steps, bulleted checklists, charts), as well as playlists (as mentioned in Chapter 6) to make it easier for students to process what they are expected to do and make.

Supports that are built into the structure (i.e., process) of a product's creation offer guidance and assist students on their path to success (macro-differentiation; see Chapter 7). What kind of scaffolds will you build in that allow all students to benefit—understanding what is expected in the product, planning for their work, moving through various stages of development, mastering content and skills, expressing their ideas, and refining their work? Then consider what aspects of the process you might need to adjust or adapt for individual students or groups (micro-differentiation) by considering the following:

- Which students will need additional personalized criteria for success?
- What kind of collaboration, oversight, or review will different groups of students need?
- Can there be alternative timelines, audiences, or methods for displaying the final product? If so, how will these alternatives be communicated or negotiated?

As illustrated by Tomlinson's DI "equalizer" (2017a; see Chapter 7), some students need more structured directions and clearly defined problems, which means taking a smaller leap; others can work more independently and address "fuzzier" problems that present more risk. The degree of independence you expect of students will vary. You might ask groups of students to check in with you at different stages (more often or less often); a few students might benefit from complete autonomy. The pacing involved in creating a product can be flexible, too, with some students spending longer on certain tasks and design aspects.

The **tools** you make available for student learning must add value to students' efforts. You want to select tools that are motivating, inspire creativity, and facilitate student expression, not those that cause students to waste time or misplace energy. You may need to establish procedures to ensure the tools are not a distraction (see Chapter 2) and to assess whether students have the support and knowledge to use these tools productively.

Use Examples and Rubrics

The learning product is supposed to give every student a chance to learn more and display the breadth and depth of their accomplishments. For this goal to be achieved, it is critical that students understand the product's purpose, including

- What learning it will display,
- What skills it will apply,
- How it will deepen learning,
- What other capacities it will help them develop, and
- How it will be assessed.

This transparency instills trust between the students and teacher, which in turn reduces anxiety during the creation of the product, making the experience of producing the work more enjoyable and improving its overall quality. It also enables students to address the intended goals for the product in its creation.

Examples and rubrics can make the "target" (i.e., the final product) more visible for students and therefore more attainable. One method of using these is to ask students to review the instructions and then explore and assess the rubric and one or more examples. This might be followed by a class discussion. The goal is to expand what students understand about the product they are being asked to create—especially what is involved in its creation and what it should express about their learning. Even in situations when it is unwise to share examples with students, they still benefit from seeing and discussing the rubric.

Teachers frequently use rubrics to expedite their grading process, but students benefit when they can see and use rubrics during the creation of their product. Rubrics identify what is essential to include in the product—the criteria make this clear. The performance indicators remove some of the "guess work" students do to understand what factors determine quality (see Figure 8.1).

When reviewing rubrics with students, point out why each criterion is included, how it is important, and how it relates to the content being studied. Suggest ways—and ask students to share approaches or provide examples, too—to address the criteria in the product. Explaining the performance indicators helps students understand the distinctions among different levels of mastery (and grading). You also want the rubric to distinguish between more important criteria—in the teamwork video, the first four criteria—and less important criteria (e.g., credits, creativity, production quality).

Other options include asking students to help construct the rubric based on the goals of the product, asking them to come up with prompts that a generative AI tool could use to create the rubric, or comparing student- or AI-created rubrics to a rubric you've developed. Offering input about the criteria for evaluation and levels of quality promotes students' comprehension and ownership. This activity helps students understand the needs of the current assignment and the various ways it aligns to the content or standards addressed during instruction. It also supports a general understanding of how rubrics promote more accurate and equitable assessment.

You can incorporate rubrics during all stages of a product's development, not just at the beginning and end. Applying the rubric to drafts in a product's formative stages results in a better product. When students consider whether their work is "stacking up," they cultivate their capacity for

FIGURE 8.1
Sample Rubric: Teamwork Video

Criteria	Great	Good	Needs Improvement
Concept of teamwork	The video addresses the general concept of what teamwork is completely, accurately, and effectively.	The video addresses the general concept of what teamwork is but does so incompletely or ineffectively.	The video does not address the general concept of teamwork.
Aspects of teamwork and their importance	The video introduces and correctly and effectively defines 2 key aspects of teamwork.	• The video either correctly or effectively introduces 2 key aspects of teamwork, but not both. • The video does not fully explain the importance of 2 key aspects of teamwork.	• The video does not introduce 2 key aspects of teamwork. • The video incorrectly or ineffectively introduces 2 key aspects of teamwork. It does not explain their importance.
Ways to develop teamwork	The video provides specific and practical ideas about how a team member can develop their capacity for teamwork.	• The video provides ideas about how teamwork can be developed, but these are not specific or practical. • The video does not provide additional information or resources.	The video does not provide ideas about how to develop a capacity for teamwork.
Illustration of concept	Effectively tells a story about a team or player in the real world that communicates important lessons about teamwork in a way that enhances the video.	• Tells a story about a team or player in the real world, but ineffectively. • The video does not communicate important lessons about teamwork in a way that enhances the video.	• Tells a story but is not based in the real world. • Tells a story that does not address teamwork.

Credits	First names of the group members and last initial are provided and shared with a creative or fun effect.	• Names of the group members are provided but do not conform to guidelines to protect the identity of students. • There is no creative or fun effect.	The names of the group members are not provided in the credits.
Creativity	There is ample evidence of efforts to exercise creativity (e.g., including humor, storytelling, pop-culture references). These enhance the quality of the video.	There is some evidence of efforts to exercise creativity (e.g., including humor, storytelling, pop-culture references). These enhance the quality of the video.	There is little or no evidence of efforts to exercise creativity or these creative efforts do not enhance the quality of the video.
Production quality	The video has excellent production quality.* Audio is audible and clear. Video is focused and not distractingly wobbly. Content can be understood with little or no effort. *The video does not have to be perfect, but it should support someone understanding the content!	The video has good production quality. The content is able to be understood with a small amount of effort.	The video has poor production quality. It is difficult to watch and learn from.

self-analysis. Peers and teachers can also offer formative evaluation using the rubric.

Remember, too, that you may need to differentiate rubrics. Similar to the layout of the video rubric, you could separate rubrics into required and optional criteria, or highlight specific criteria for certain groups of students. Another method is to include optional criteria that challenge students to deeper learning and higher levels of synthesis, expression, and skill.

Assign Products That Are Culturally Responsive

The Center for Collaborative Education (2017) created a checklist that teachers can use to evaluate assessments for bias, stereotyping, fairness, cultural responsiveness, and presentation of potentially controversial material. We recommend using it to evaluate product assignments under development.

There are a couple of ways to factor cultural responsiveness into product design. You could ask students to draw a connection between a product they create and their lives, community, culture, and background, or you might choose a product task that deliberately builds students' cultural competence—focuses them on learning about or expressing pride in their culture or others' cultures. Consider using web conferencing tools like Zoom to foster cross-cultural interaction, collaboration, and evaluation with students who reside in other states or countries as well as with content area experts and professionals. And don't forget to explore options for virtual field trips or access to digital archives of primary source material available from museums all over the world.

It is important for teachers to encourage students to engage critically with the world around them and develop bridges that connect students' backgrounds and cultures to academic skills and concepts. Doing so also engages students in critical reflection about their own lives and society.

Incorporate Student Voice and Choice

Although student input (i.e., voice) and freedom to make selections (i.e., choice) are important in all aspects of differentiated instruction, they are exceptionally important in the design of products. This is because products are culminating expressions of student learning that are intended to result in ownership of the knowledge and skills that have been gained. Designing products that incorporate student voice and choice makes them more inspirational and ultimately creates the conditions for students to show what they know in the best way possible.

Much of what we have discussed in this chapter describes how to design product assignments that incorporate student voice and choice, such as letting students choose from different formats (e.g., advertisement, diagram, role-play) or tools. The format a product takes and the technologies that may be used to create it should reflect what students find relevant, interesting, and inspiring. When the topic or content being incorporated for a product appears to be less interesting to students, pair it with a more interesting format or technology. You can also ask students to suggest formats and technologies they would like to use. When they do, be sure to honor their preferences.

Design Authentic, Real-World Products

Research shows that making connections to the real world is important to student learning (Bransford et al., 2000). It's a way for students to demonstrate skills needed in real life or in the workforce; knowing that what they are creating has real-world applications or audiences can provide additional motivation. "Real-world products" are those that might be used or created by others outside school such as designing a school playground, making a video of local landmarks, producing a guide to star gazing, or creating a kit to analyze the pH level of rain in the neighborhood. Some real-world products organically incorporate digital tools, and others do not.

Using Digital Tools to Address the 4Es and Respond to Barriers

When designing learning products, you need to balance opportunities for student learning and assessment (e.g., development of skills, deepening knowledge, opportunities to self-monitor and develop independence) with the practical constraints of time, student ability, and resources. With so many options for products that might be created, which digital technologies might be the most valuable addition to your teacher tool set?

Share and Showcase Products Virtually

Students should feel that the work they do at school matters. Endless practice with no opportunity for performance (i.e., sharing their accomplishments with others) will discourage even the most diligent and dedicated student. Having an authentic audience can be very motivating. Students benefit from having peers, friends, family members, and even willing outside experts view, critique, and affirm their efforts. When selecting digital tools for the design of a product, prioritize those that make it easy to share.

This high-tech option has the affordance of making the sharing process easier (in most cases); rather than scheduling an in-school "museum night" that not all families can attend, set up a website (e.g., VoiceThread) that others can visit any time. Visitors can leave an audio or text message; other tools enable them to overlay annotations (e.g., markings or text) on students' work. Students can log on and hear or read the feedback they have received, gaining affirmation and encouragement (and possibly also additional learning) from their audience. Artsonia, an online art portfolio, not only allows students' products to be uploaded and receive comments, but it also has a "gift shop" where audience members can order merchandise with students' original artwork on it.

As we've mentioned before, when considering these types of high-tech options, you want to ensure equitable access. If there are students in your class who lack home access to the technology tools and communications networks required to complete the product and cannot secure access via a take-home device or the public library, either provide sufficient class time for product work and alternate activities to do at home or revamp the product assignment to eliminate any inequitable components.

Use Flexible Formats and Tools

Not all product formats and the tools for creating them are created equal. Some offer additional power and advantage in a differentiated classroom because they are more flexible for customization by students, more easily able to promote and present student learning, and more readily integrated across grade level and subject area. Formats that are open-ended and promote student expression and creativity work best for most students, provided there is enough structure to ensure they are meeting the product development guidelines. Tools for creating products should be easy to use and flexible in what they can achieve.

One such format is the paperslide video (McCammon, 2019). It uses simple materials and requires only paper, markers, and a video recorder. Like multimedia presentations such as Google Slides or PowerPoint, paperslide videos blend text and images; unlike such presentations, the slides are created on paper. One affordance of paperslides is that they require only a small amount of technical expertise and technology, but they have a big effect on how much, how well, and how enthusiastically students learn—making them a low-tech, high-impact practice. Produced independently or in groups to respond to the instructions and rubric, paperslides can convey the breadth and depth of student learning. The digital format offers some additional affordances, including capturing live presentations that can be viewed at another time, in another location. Making paperslide videos is fun for students; they offer tremendous scope for creativity and imagination. Many of our learners not only like using technology-based tools but also like expressing their ideas in multimedia formats and using real-world tools while doing academic learning. Paperslide video products simultaneously allow students to engage in content-area learning while developing the "4C super-skills": communication, collaboration, creativity, and critical thinking (Kivunja, 2015).

Note that the process of creating the paperslide video (see Figure 8.2) does not include editing. This is because editing requires time, additional resources, and advanced technical skills, which can be a constraint for other types of multimedia presentations students use for a product. Editing also sets high, and often unrealistic, expectations for production quality that can hinder the experimentation, risk taking, and creativity that paperslide videos promote.

There are some rules or conventions that are popular when creating paperslide videos. First, make sure the video presents the content accurately. The quality of the video will have a lot to do with whether the information it presents is clear, accurate, and detailed. Second, the video should be creative (e.g., with images, humor, pop-culture references, special effects). Video creators should endeavor to make the video interesting, fun, and engaging for their classmates.

FIGURE 8.2
Process of Creating a Paperslide Video

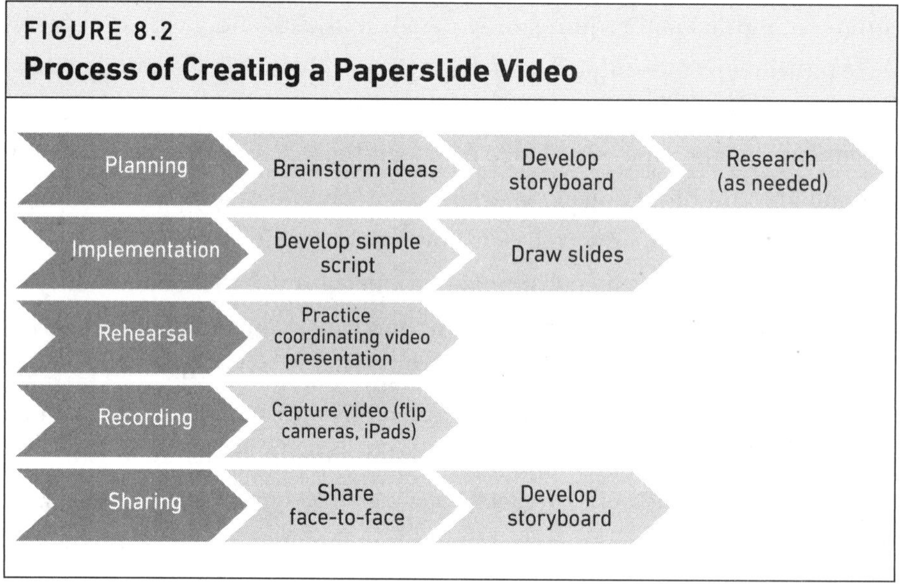

Expedite the Grading Process

The time and labor involved in grading unique products is one excuse teachers use for not incorporating products more often in student learning. However, this need not be the case. There are products that both provide a healthy challenge for students and streamline the volume of material that must be reviewed when being evaluated by the teacher. Products that require students to distill ideas and information into more succinct formats (e.g., summaries, diagrams, logos) will hone students' communication skills while economizing the work of an evaluator (whether teacher or classmate).

Infographics, previously mentioned, display different types of knowledge in a visual format. Infographics can communicate

- Conceptual knowledge, using diagrams;
- Procedural knowledge, using lists;
- Factual knowledge, using textboxes; and

- Metacognitive knowledge, using images or links to additional resources (e.g., videos).

Infographics tend to be both short (one or two pages at most) and present condensed information that responds to the teacher's instructions. Software (e.g., Microsoft Publisher) and online tools (e.g., Canva, Easelly) make it easy for students to log in, open a blank page, and use embedded features to incorporate images, shapes, and text. Students benefit from the parameter of parsimony in this type of product and learn to make better choices about the limited space available.

Another condensed format for a product that challenges students and saves time grading is a **PechaKucha** (Japanese for "chit-chat"). Originated in Japan by architects Astrid Klein and Mark Dytham, this is a 20-second, 20-slide presentation (PechaKucha, n.d.). Like other short-format presentations (e.g., an elevator pitch), PechaKucha is a way to tell a story or share information in an informative, concise, yet enthusiastic way. They tend to be highly visual and incorporate many images and diagrams. Students can share their presentations in a live, synchronous format or record them and share them asynchronously. An affordance of this method for assessment is that it can be viewed by multiple people at the same time, inside or outside the classroom. A constraint is that PechaKucha lectures may be challenging for the youngest learners to storyboard and create.

Ensure Equity Through Offering Choice

Students differ in many ways—not the least of which is in how comfortable they feel creating and displaying the proficiencies that are part of a product. Delivering a live presentation might make students anxious or uncomfortable. If so, they may not accurately display their achievements. This is another reason digital tools can improve the design of differentiated products. When it is appropriate given the goals for the product, the expectations for learners, and other contextual factors (e.g., technological availability, time), give students options for presenting their product—live, in person, or a pre-recorded, canned format. This makes the assignment more equitable.

Presentations can range from simple slide shows or video recordings made with a tablet or on a computer or smartphone, to a more complex screencast. Some students will appreciate having the option to decide how they want to appear and communicate in their presentations. It may be more equitable (and possibly also more effective and fun) to allow students to use a representation of themselves instead of an actual video or still image. Avatar tools (e.g., Voki) make it easy for students to create a "talking head" avatar. Although such methods of using digital tools offer the affordance of making presentations more equitable for most students, teachers will want to consider their use carefully to ensure they are, indeed, equitable for all students. It's always important to consider balancing students' preferences with their need to challenge themselves and develop interpersonal skills.

Questions for Reflection

- What kinds of choices do you offer students in product assignments?
- Which product formats that you use are most effective in deepening students' skills and knowledge? Are there others that might better demonstrate student learning?
- How do you scaffold product assignments so students can demonstrate and reflect on progress?
- How might product assignments reflect culturally responsive instruction?
- How do you incorporate formative and summative assessment in product assignments?

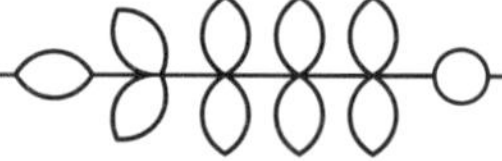

9

Sustaining the Work of Differentiated Instruction

This chapter covers…

- Why differentiated instruction is so relevant today.
- When, how often, and how best to innovate with differentiation and technology.
- The professional development that best supports teachers committed to designing more equitable, efficient, effective, and engaging instruction.
- How digital tools influence differentiation, teachers' ability to differentiate, and continued professional learning in the future.

Teachers have many reasons for pursuing a career in education. For some, it is a deep love of humanity and a desire to usher young people through important developmental stages. For others, it is the opportunity to pass on their passion for a particular subject or for learning in general. Still other teachers are drawn to the idea of building a better society by influencing the formation of caring, concerned, and capable citizens. For most, it is a combination of all these factors.

Regardless of why you chose this profession, remaining in it is more rewarding when you successfully meet the job's many and varied demands. Understanding how to integrate design and technology tools to better achieve the goals of differentiation contributes to that success.

How Is Differentiated Instruction Relevant Today?

In a profession where attention spans are short and new professional development fads are always appearing like a flavor of the month, the continued prominence of differentiated instruction is not just impressive—it's remarkable. Why differentiation has only increased in popularity during a 20-year period in which so much else in the field has cycled in and out is worthy of deeper consideration.

Teachers stick with differentiation because it works. It empowers them as professionals, giving them a reliable means to support a variety of learners working to meet challenging and changing standards and helps them to prioritize the relational aspects of teaching that power all learning. Students appreciate differentiation because it places their uniqueness at the center of learning; experiences in a differentiated classroom help them develop the skills, knowledge, relationships, and independence they need for both short-term and long-term success.

Differentiation is a growing trend in society at large, one that promises to remain for the foreseeable future. Examining its role in contemporary life validates differentiated instruction's current and continued importance in the field of education and can provide insight for the directions it might take in the future.

You can see differentiation in the design and success of many popular chain restaurants that offer a range of options to cater to customers' tastes. First, you decide if you want a bowl, a salad, or a wrap, and then you examine the range of carefully selected and sourced options and let the restaurant staff put together a unique meal to your exact specifications. You can also pull out your smartphone and create one-of-a-kind gifts through photo merchandise services or order unique, personalized sports apparel. Differentiation is a means through which the world can accommodate personal differences and tastes.

If differentiation evolves in education in parallel with other fields, educators can expect the development of new tools that will allow more powerful and more nuanced identification of individual differences. As artificial intelligence and learning analytics continue to develop, new administrative, operational, and pedagogical technologies will make it easier to gather, analyze, and monitor students' performance data. With better information on students' patterns of difficulty, teachers can provide guidance and support more readily and effectively. Better identification of students' differences can also be expected to give rise to new tools for addressing these differences. Increasingly powerful virtual assistants and chatbots will be available to support not only the teaching–learning process but also the design of it. Teachers and students will want to work together to determine when and how they can best supplement and augment the work of a differentiated classroom.

As technological options for supporting the many aspects of differentiated instruction expand and become increasingly complex in their uses and effects, a design orientation to practice will allow teachers to marshal the powerful resources available in the most influential ways. Professional development and a commitment to continual learning will be critical to their success.

Progressing with Differentiation

Differentiated instruction and the ways in which a teacher with a design orientation and digital tools can transform its implementation offers so many possibilities that it's hard to know where to begin. Committing to the goals of differentiation initiates a long-term process that can extend across various stages of your career. Figure 9.1 illustrates a continuum of progress that you might experience as you develop proficiency with differentiated instruction over time. Although every teacher is unique and will experience their own growth progression, it can be helpful to ask yourself where you are now with the many different dimensions of differentiated instruction practice. Where do you want to go? In what ways will you benefit by challenging yourself (and not just your students) to progress, become more proficient, and overcome obstacles? It might also be helpful to benchmark yourself to other professional assessments, such as the CEEDAR Center's (n.d.) *Differentiated Instruction Self-Assessment* or the Montgomery County (Maryland) Public Schools' reproduction of a rubric developed by Tomlinson and Hockett (n.d.).

Sometimes teachers who are new to differentiation and educational design think that every lesson's content, process, product, and environment must be designed to differentiate based on readiness, interest, *and*

FIGURE 9.1

A Continuum of Growth in Differentiated Instruction Proficiency

Area	Beginning	Developing	Refining
Assessment	The teacher incorporates some summative assessment.	The teacher incorporates some pre-assessment, formative, and summative assessment in teaching.	The teacher • Has a DI assessment plan that incorporates pre-, formative, and summative assessment; • Pre-assesses students routinely in advance to plan better instruction; • Uses high- and low-tech approaches to promote equity; and • Incorporates digital tools effectively to address differentiated instruction goals.
Classroom management	The teacher has a reactive plan for classroom management.	The teacher has both proactive and reactive plans for classroom management.	Classroom procedures are known to the teacher and the students and are rehearsed and practiced to the point that few problems exist.
Communication	Parents are unaware of differentiation strategies.	• Parents are aware of differentiation strategies and invited to communicate. • There is a communication plan to ensure that all involved know how to be a supportive part of the differentiated learning community.	Parents receive regular communication about strategies being used in class and tips for what to do at home to support their child's learning efforts.
Learning community	The teacher strives to make the classroom a space where all students are respected and encouraged to learn about themselves and take responsibility for the success of others.	The teacher has begun to create a classroom community.	The teacher • Intentionally builds a community that incorporates a collective vision of success resulting from each student supporting one another; and • Includes extended members of the learning community in intentional ways that are supported by digital tools.

Frequency of DI implementation	The teacher tries to plan one lesson using differentiation strategies once a week.	The teacher plans more than one lesson using differentiation strategies in a week.	The teacher routinely plans more than one daily lesson using DI strategies.
DI strategies	The teacher uses micro-differentiation strategies: • Choices of books or other resources • Homework/project options • Varied scaffolding • Flexible grouping • Plan for quick finishers	The teacher incorporates macro-differentiation strategies: • Tiered activities and labs • Multiple texts • Alternative assessments • Literature circles • Flexible reading formats • The teacher also uses micro-differentiation strategies as needed.	The teacher uses a variety of strategies depending on what works best to support student learning: • Makes choice a routine component of instruction; • Empowers students to know their own needs and self-advocate; • Uses learning centers; • Uses tiered assignments, products, and rubrics; and • Uses agendas.
Instructional groupings	The teacher primarily uses whole-class instructional grouping.	The teacher uses both whole-class grouping and small-group instruction.	The teacher uses • Whole-class/one-size-fits-all instructional grouping with special attention for certain groups; and • Flexible grouping (centers, stations)

(continued)

FIGURE 9.1—(*continued*)

A Continuum of Growth in Differentiated Instruction Proficiency

Area	Beginning	Developing	Refining
Cooperation with others	The teacher most often works alone but has begun to seek out connections with other teachers who are also using differentiated instruction strategies.	The teacher • Shares ideas with others attempting to differentiate; and • Has begun to start a self-study group in the district.	The teacher • Plans in collaboration with other teachers who are differentiating and turns to them for support and peer evaluation; • Is part of a professional learning community sharing plans, ideas, critiques, materials; and • Works with colleagues at school to further differentiation efforts.
Pre-assessment	The teacher does not routinely pre-assess students.	The teacher pre-assesses students periodically	The teacher • Pre-assesses students routinely to plan better instruction; • Uses high- and low-tech approaches to promote equity; and • Incorporates digital tools to support pre-assessment efforts.
Professional development	The teacher • Attends conferences and other presentations focused on DI. • Reads books about DI independently.	The teacher • Belongs to a discussion group that focuses on differentiation issues; • Is working to develop relationships with differentiating colleagues and community of practice; and • Participates in online class about DI.	The teacher • Has read extensively about DI; • Has taken courses about DI; • Is part of an online book group that reads and discusses DI; and • Presents at conferences and/or leads professional development about DI.

learning profile. This approach is tremendously difficult (if not impossible); it's *not* one a seasoned differentiator would recommend. Attempting to differentiate everything all the time is a ticket to teacher and student burnout.

Teachers functioning as educational designers should be strategic in their practice as a whole. This means both looking at the design of individual lessons and developing long- and short-term goals for improving their use of differentiated instruction. It is important to balance these goals with other goals, including those focused on sustaining impact across the school year.

One rule of thumb that helps to determine when to differentiate is "Do it when you *can* and do it when it *counts*." This principle has some flexibility in how it can be understood and applied, but it offers teachers a way of thinking about when to push themselves for growth in their ability to innovate—whether that be with differentiation or technology or both.

Innovate When You Can

Teachers striving to design various aspects of their practice to achieve the goals of differentiation for their students are always functioning as designers. As they serve their students, they make intentional choices about what they choose to do and choose *not* to do. These choices are made realistically in relation to their goals and different contextual parameters (e.g., time, energy, attention, resources).

It's important to prioritize how to spend your energies and to allocate the resources available to you (e.g., teaching time, tools, energy) in the most purposeful, productive ways. There will be times when you can innovate more fruitfully—these times are ripe or appropriate for trying something new, taking greater risks, or making a bigger stretch to incorporate something sophisticated from your instructional repertoire. As an independent professional, decide when it is possible to innovate and when it might not make sense to do so.

You may be able to differentiate instruction relatively easily when the following factors apply:

- The content standards are already familiar;
- High-quality materials for instruction have already been developed and can be used as a foundation for creating different versions;

- Additional instructional assistance is available from a classroom aide or volunteers;
- Extra time is available; and
- The content, process, product, and environment are all well suited to going deeper or allowing student choice.

You'll be best positioned to innovate with technology when the following conditions are met:

- There is plenty of instructional time available;
- You have additional planning time;
- Equipment is available for technology-integrated lessons;
- You have the skill and knowledge required for implementing digital tools;
- Additional people are available to assist with lesson implementation;
- There is the ability to remediate if the lesson "bombs" or students have difficulty; and
- Technology addresses any of the 4Es.

Innovate When It Counts

There are times when extra effort can really make a difference in the outcome of instruction in general or for certain learners. Innovating during these moments counts more and thus justifies greater effort.

There are critical understandings teachers develop as they transition from novice to expert. One is an awareness of their students' needs and the differences among them. Another is an understanding of which curriculum standards present the most difficulty for students. Whether there is a developmental disconnect between the students and the learning to be addressed or limited materials available to teach a particular concept, successful teachers identify which standards are most difficult to teach. There are more and less efficient ways of teaching the same standards.

You might differentiate because it counts when

- Learners with exceptional needs can be included in potentially powerful ways;
- There is a need to "hook" students with something novel to encourage interest in a "dull" topic;

- The concepts will be especially challenging for the students you teach; or
- Distractions and interruptions are expected.

You might decide to incorporate digital tools because it counts when

- The available digital tools will promote more equitable, efficient, effective, or engaging instruction (i.e., they incorporate the 4Es);
- The digital tools being integrated will address barriers to frequent, consistent, and powerful differentiation; or
- The digital tools can support differentiation via content, process, product, or environment.

Continuing Professional Learning

Designers across different fields have a lot in common. Not only do they possess a design mindset, skill set, and tool set, but they also pursue ongoing professional learning. Much of their acquired knowledge comes from experience and reflection upon that experience. As you continue to learn about your students, make decisions based on careful analysis, and implement and learn the outcome of your efforts, reflection can help you become a more effective and resourceful teacher. However, designers also take advantage of other valuable methods for professional learning, including (1) participating in communities of practice, (2) connecting to professional organizations, (3) and engaging with high-quality books and other resources.

Communities of Practice

In a community of practice, professionals come together around a concern or a passion for something they do and learn how to do it better as they interact regularly (Lave & Wenger, 1991). Communities might be organized at the school or local level or distributed across a wider network (e.g., nationally, globally); they meet with different degrees of frequency (e.g., weekly, monthly), in person or virtually (e.g., videoconferencing, discussion boards). Members exchange ideas, resources, research, and materials that help grow the knowledge of group members individually and collectively. Communities also build a sense of unity and purpose and can offer social support.

The advantage of a community of practice is that there is a common understanding and orientation that bonds individual practitioners to one another and elevates their work. Depending on where you are situated, you may be able to join a community of practice for designing to differentiate. Finding communities of practice focusing on differentiated instruction in your local area might be appealing. There is definitely a benefit in being able to meet colleagues in person for a cup of coffee while also exchanging tips, sharing resources, and growing a professional network. Your school district central office, local Educational Services Center (ESC), or a regional professional development provider may know if these groups exist.

Another option would be to search the internet to see if there are communities of practice that would be attractive to you involving professionals from near and far. Facebook groups, Reddit communities and subcommunities, and professional social media networks may present options that work for you. Participating in such online networks may be easier than meeting in person; it's more flexible and convenient. You can expect the personalities, experiences, and ideas shared to range broadly.

A third option would be to start your own community of practice in either format. You'll want to identify your goals for your community, make sure to name it carefully (so that others can find it), and advertise it in ways that work for your onsite or virtual community. It always helps to network with your current professional contacts and take advantage of existing means of publicity, such as teacher newsletters, blogs, and the like.

Professional Organizations

The field of education has benefitted from professional organizations centered around different missions or interests. We are fortunate to have many fine organizations such as ASCD + ISTE, the National Education Association, Learning Forward, and others that publish written and electronic materials for their membership; hold annual in-person and virtual gatherings; and offer curated resources, newsletters, and other resources that benefit professional educators. One of the greatest benefits of these groups is that they bring professionals together from a wide variety of backgrounds around shared concerns and promote continual development and growth.

High-Quality Professional Development

Although there are many professional development opportunities teachers can take advantage of, many of which are offered online, not all professional development is high quality. According to Darling-Hammond and colleagues (2017), effective professional development

- Focuses on content;
- Incorporates active learning based on learning theory;
- Supports collaboration;
- Uses models and modeling of effective practice;
- Provides coaching and expert support;
- Offers opportunities for feedback and reflection; and
- Can be sustained long term.

When choosing professional development opportunities, it helps to keep these elements in mind to ensure that what is chosen is most effective and beneficial. Possible sources of professional development besides courses or workshops include quality books and other resources, such as online blogs, newsletters, YouTube channels, and more.

* * *

It is ironic but not surprising that teachers who spend so much time supporting their students' learning find it so difficult to attend to their own growth and development. The best educators are lifelong learners, and learning has intrinsic benefits beyond mastery of specific subject matter or skills. It is enjoyable, engages our curiosity about the world we live in, and incites our wonder. It helps us discover and know ourselves (e.g., one's special gifts and interests, as well as limitations) and develop meaningful relationships. And learning can expose us to new ways of thinking and viewpoints that transform how we interact with one another and the world around us.

All of these benefits multiply in a well-managed differentiated classroom led by teachers who continually build their differentiation skills and incorporate up-to-date technology to design more engaging, efficient, effective, and equitable learning.

Questions for Reflection

- Based on what you have learned about differentiated instruction in this book, in what areas do you still need to develop and grow? How will you pursue this growth?
- Design a professional development plan that identifies short- and long-term goals and objectives. Then, plan out when and how you will achieve these goals and objectives with specific outcomes and deadlines.

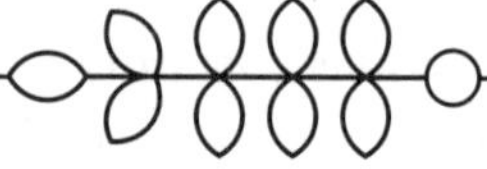

References

Anderson, L. W., Krathwohl, D. R., Airasian, P. W., Cruikshank, K. A., Mayer, R. E., Pintrich, P. R., Raths, J., & Wittrock, M. C. (2001). *A taxonomy for learning, teaching, and assessing.* Longman.

Atkin, J. M., & Karplus R. (1962). Discovery of invention? *Science Teaching, 29,* 45–51. https://www.jstor.org/stable/24146536

Beaty-O'Ferrall, M. E., Green, A., & Hanna, F. (2010). Classroom management strategies for difficult students: Promoting change through relationships. *Middle School Journal, 41*(4), 4–11. https://files.eric.ed.gov/fulltext/EJ887746.pdf

Bransford, J. D., Brown, A. L., & Cocking, R. R. (Eds.). (2000). *How people learn: Brain, mind, experience and school.* National Academies Press. https://nap.nationalacademies.org/read/9853/chapter/1

Bybee, R., & Landes, N. M. (1990). Science for life and living: An elementary school science program from Biological Sciences Curriculum Study (BSCS). *The American Biology Teacher, 52*(2), 92–98. https://doi.org/10.2307/4449042

CAST. (2024). *About universal design for learning.* https://www.cast.org/impact/universal-design-for-learning-udl

CEEDAR Center. (n.d.). *What is differentiated instruction (DI) self-assessment?* https://ceedar.education.ufl.edu/wp-content/uploads/2016/11/FIN-DI-Self-Assessment-Tool-ns.pdf

Center for Collaborative Education. (2017). *Fairness, bias, and cultural-responsiveness checklist.* https://studentsatthecenterhub.org/wp-content/uploads/Fairness-Bias-and-Cultural-Responsiveness-Checklist.pdf

Churches, A. (2008). Bloom's digital taxonomy. https://www.researchgate.net/publication/228381038_Bloom's_Digital_Taxonomy

Cobb, J. A. (1972). Relationship of discrete classroom behaviors to fourth-grade academic achievement. *Journal of Educational Psychology, 63*(1), 74–80. https://doi.org/10.1037/h0032247

Darling-Hammond, L., Hyler, M. E., Gardner, M., & Espinoza, D. (2017, May). *Effective teacher professional development* (Research Brief). Learning Policy Institute. https://doi.org/10.54300/122.311

Dewey, J. (1933). *How we think: A restatement of the relation of reflective thinking to the educative process.* Heath.

Dodge, B. (1997). *Some thoughts about WebQuests.* https://jotamac.typepad.com/jotamacs_weblog/files/WebQuests.pdf

Flipped Learning Network. (2014). *The four pillars of F-L-I-P.* https://flippedlearning.org/wp-content/uploads/2016/07/FLIP_handout_FNL_Web.pdf

Finn, J. D., Pannozzo, G. M., & Voelkl, K. E. (1995, May). Disruptive and inattentive withdrawn behavior and achievement among fourth graders. *Elementary School Journal, 95,* 421–454. https://doi.org/10.1086/461853

Finn, J. D., & Rock, D. A. (1997). Academic success among students at risk for school failure. *Journal of Applied Psychology, 82,* 221-234. https://doi.org/10.1037/0021-9010.82.2.221

Fulton, M. K., & Reil. M. (1999, April 30). Professional development through learning communities. *Edutopia Online.* https://www.edutopia.org/professional-development-through-learning-communities

Gardner, H. (1999). *Intelligence reframed: Multiple intelligences for the 21st century.* Basic Books.

Gay, G. (2018). *Culturally responsive teaching: Theory, research, and practice* (Multicultural Education Series, 3rd ed.). Teachers College Press.

Gay, G. (2023). *Educating for equity and excellence: Enacting culturally responsive teaching.* Teachers College Press.

Goddard, Y. L., Goddard, R. D., Bailes, L. P, & Nichols, R. (2019). From school leadership to differentiated instruction: A pathway to student learning in schools. *The Elementary School Journal, 120*(2), 197–219. https://doi.org/10.1086/705827

Gonzalez, J. (2016, September 4). *Using playlists to differentiate instruction.* https://www.cultofpedagogy.com/student-playlists-differentiation/

Harper, B., & Milman, N. B. (2016). One-to-one technology in K–12 classrooms: A review of the literature from 2004 through 2014. *Journal of Research on Technology and Education, 48*(2), 129–142. https://doi.org/10.1080/15391523.2016.1146564

Hattie, J., & Timperley, H. (2007). The power of feedback. *Review of Educational Research, 77*(1), 81–112. https://doi.org/10.3102/003465430298487

Jonassen, D. H. (1996). *Computers in the classroom: Mindtools for critical thinking.* Merrill/Prentice Hall.

Kalir, R., & Garcia, A. (2021). *Annotation* (MIT Press Essential Knowledge series). MIT Press.

Kilbane, C. R., & Milman, N. B. (2003). *What every school leader should know about digital portfolios.* Pearson.

Kilbane, C. R., & Milman, N. B. (2014). *Teaching models: Designing instruction for 21st century learners.* Pearson.

Kilbane, C. R., & Milman, N. B. (2023, June). Differentiated learning and technology: A powerful combination. *Educational Leadership, 80*(9). https://www.ascd.org/el/articles/differentiated-learning-and-technology-a-powerful-combination

Kivunja, C. (2015). Exploring the pedagogical meaning and implications of the 4Cs "super skills" for the 21st century through Bruner's 5E lenses of knowledge construction to improve pedagogies of the new learning paradigm. *Creative Education, 6*(2), 224–239. https://doi.org/10.4236/ce.2015.62021

Lahaderne, H. M. (1968). Attitudinal and intellectual correlates of attention: A study of four sixth-grade classrooms. *Journal of Educational Psychology, 59*(5), 320–324. https://doi.org/10.1037/h0026223

Lave, J., & Wenger, E. (1991). *Situated learning: Legitimate peripheral participation.* Cambridge University Press. https://doi.org/10.1017/CBO9780511815355

Marshall, T. R. (2022, November). The promise, power, and practice of student agency. *Educational Leadership, 80*(3), 33–38. https://www.ascd.org/el/articles/the-promise-power-and-practice-of-student-agency

Martlett, D. (n.d.). *A guide to the R.A.F.T. writing strategy across content areas.* Learning-Focused. https://learningfocused.com/a-guide-to-the-r-a-f-t-writing-strategy-across-content-areas/

Mavidou, A., & Kakana, D. (2019). Differentiated instruction in practice: Curriculum adjustments in kindergarten. *Creative Education, 10*(3), 535–554. https://doi.org/10.4236/ce.2019.103039

McCammon, L. (2019). Technology in the classroom: Simple "paperslide" videos are an easy way to reinforce learning. *Page One, 40*(3), 28–29. https://issuu.com/pagemagazines/docs/page_one_jan_feb_2019

Merrill, S., & Gonser, S. (2021, September 16). The importance of student choice across all grade levels. *Edutopia.* https://www.edutopia.org/article/importance-student-choice-across-all-grade-levels/

Miley, F., & Read, A. (2011). Using word clouds to develop proactive learners. *Journal of the Scholarship of Teaching and Learning, 11*(2), 91–110. https://files.eric.ed.gov/fulltext/EJ932148.pdf

Milman, N. B., Carlson-Bancroft, A., & Vanden Boogart, A. (2014). Examining differentiation and utilization of iPads across content areas in an independent, preK-fourth grade elementary school. *Computers in the Schools, 31*(3), 119–133. https://doi.org/10.1080/07380569.2014.931776

Milman, N. B., & Vanden Boogart, A. (2024). The promise of differentiating reading and writing instruction across content areas with 1:1 iPads in an elementary school. *Computers in the Schools.* https://doi.org/10.1080/07380569.2024.2337649

Mishra, P., & Koehler, M. J. (2006). Technological pedagogical content knowledge: A framework for teacher knowledge. *Teachers College Record, 108*(6), 1017–1054. https://doi.org/10.1111/j.1467-9620.2006.00684.x

Paricio, D., Herrera, M., Rodrigo, M.F., & Viguer, P. (2020). Association between group identification at school and positive youth development: Moderating role of rural and urban contexts. *Frontiers in Psychology, 11,* 1–14. https://doi.org/10.3389/fpsyg.2020.01971

PechaKucha. (n.d.). *What is a 20x20 PechaKucha?* https://www.pechakucha.com/about

Puentedura, R. (2013). SAMR model: Substitution, augmentation, modification, redefinition. https://d1pf6s1cgoc6y0.cloudfront.net/5fdcf2f73b804107b4fa3f2b6177affa.pdf

Reis, S. M., McCoach, D. B., Little, C. A., Muller, L. M., & Kaniskan, R. B. (2011). The effects of differentiated instruction and enrichment pedagogy on reading achievement in five elementary schools. *American Educational Research Journal, 48,* 462–501. https://doi.org/10.3102/0002831210382891

Roberts, T., & Hernandez, K. (2019). Digital access is not binary: The 5 "A's" of technology access in the Philippines. *Electronic Journal of Information Systems in Developing Countries, 85(4),* 1–14. https://doi.org/10.1002/isd2.12084

Samuels, S. J., & Turnure, J. E. (1974). Attention and reading achievement in first-grade boys and girls. *Journal of Educational Psychology, 66*(1), 29–32. https://doi.org/10.1037/h0035812

Schrock, K. (2024, July 17). Post 3: SAMR and Bloom's and tech. *Kaffeeklatch.* https://kathyschrock.net/kaffeeklatsch/samr-and-blooms-and-tech

Shulman, L. S. (1986). Those who understand: Knowledge growth in teaching. *Educational Researcher, 15*(2), 4–14. https://doi.org/10.3102/0013189X015002004

Shulman, L. S. (1987). Knowledge and teaching: Foundations of the new reform. *Harvard Educational Review, 57*(1), 1–22. https://doi.org/10.17763/haer.57.1.j463w79r56455411

Shulman, L. (1992). Ways of seeing, ways of knowing, ways of teaching, ways of learning about teaching. *Journal of Curriculum Studies, 28*(5), 393–396. https://doi.org/10.1080/0022027910230501

Taba, H., Durkin, M. C., Fraenkel, J. R., & McNaughton, A. H. (1971). *A teacher's handbook to elementary social studies: An inductive approach* (2nd ed.). Addison-Wesley.

Tomlinson, C. A. (1995). *How to differentiate instruction in mixed ability classrooms.* ASCD.

Tomlinson, C. A. (2014). *The differentiated classroom: Responding to the needs of all learners* (2nd ed.). ASCD.

Tomlinson, C. A. (2017a). *How to differentiate instruction in academically diverse classrooms* (3rd ed.). ASCD.

Tomlinson, C. A. (2017b). *Understanding differentiated instruction* (Quick Reference Guide). ASCD.

Tomlinson, C. A., & Hockett, J. (n.d.). *Look-fors in an effectively differentiated classroom.* https://www.montgomeryschoolsmd.org/siteassets/schools/high-schools/r-w/senecavalleyhs/uploadedfiles/academics/staffdev/diff-lookfors.pdf

Tomlinson, C. A., & Imbeau, M. B. (2023). *Leading and managing a differentiated classroom* (2nd ed.). ASCD.

Tomlinson, C. A., & Moon, T. (2013). *Assessment and student success in a differentiated classroom.* ASCD. https://doi.org/10.4135/9781483365633.n1

TPACK.org. (2012). Technological pedagogical content knowledge [Online image]. https://matt-koehler.com/tpack2/wp-content/uploads/2013/08/TPACK-new.png

Tseng, S.-S. (2021). The influence of teacher annotations on student learning engagement and video watching behaviors. *International Journal of Educational Technology in Higher Education, 18,* 1–17. https://doi-org.proxygw.wrlc.org/10.1186/s41239-021-00242-5

Vygotsky, L. S. (1978). *Thought and language.* MIT Press.

Wong, H. K., & Wong, R. T. (2018). *The first days of school: Becoming an effective* teacher (5th ed.). Harry K. Wong.

Zheng, L., Long, M., Zhong, L., & Gyasi, J. F. (2022). The effectiveness of technology-facilitated personalized learning on learning achievements and learning perceptions: A meta-analysis. *Education and Information Technologies, 27*(8), 11807–11830. https://doi-org.proxygw.wrlc.org/10.1007/s10639-022-11092-7

Index

The letter *f* following a page locator denotes a figure.

About the Authors

Clare Kilbane is a professor at the University of Notre Dame, where she educates future teachers, designs curriculum materials, and conducts research on education. She also serves as the director of research and development for online education at the McGrath Institute and is its senior learning designer.

Kilbane is a former elementary school teacher and has 20 years of experience working in teacher education at five institutions of higher education. A versatile scholar, she has authored many videos and multimedia products as well as more than 35 articles, book chapters, papers, and reviews. The most recent of her seven books include *Teaching Models: Designing Instruction for 21st Century Learners* (with Natalie Milman; 2014) and *The 4C's: Understanding 21st Century Skills in the Light of Faith Collaboration* (2022).

Kilbane has a degree in elementary education from the University of Dayton, a master's degree in instructional design and technology from The Ohio State University, and a doctorate in educational evaluation from the University of Virginia. She lives in South Bend, Indiana, with her family and Glen of Imaal Terriers. Contact her at ckilbane@nd.edu.

Natalie B. Milman is associate dean of the office of students at The George Washington University's Graduate School of Education and Human Development and a professor of educational technology in the online Educational Technology Leadership Program. She is also a member of the interdisciplinary Human-Technology Collaboration PhD program and research lab, a member of GW's Academy of Distinguished Teachers, and recipient of the 2017 Bender Teaching Award. Her research focuses on the design of instruction and models for the effective leadership and integration of technology at all academic levels; online student support needs, engagement, and learning; issues of diversity, inclusion, and digital equity; and the use of digital portfolios for professional development.

Milman is co-editor of the Current Practice Section of *Contemporary Issues in Technology and Teacher Education* and has published numerous journal articles. She presents frequently at conferences and is the co-author of several book chapters and books. Her most recent book with Clare Kilbane is *Teaching Models: Designing Instruction for 21st Century Learners* (2022).

Milman earned a doctorate in instructional technology from the University of Virginia's School of Education and Human Development with a specialization in preparing technology leaders. She began her career in education as a 2nd grade science specialist, mentor, and technology teacher in Los Angeles County, California. She has taught at the graduate school level since 1997 and online since 2001. She is fluent in Spanish, a first-generation Colombian American, and a first-generation BA, MA, and PhD graduate. Contact her at nmilman@gwu.edu.

Related ASCD Resources: Differentiated Instruction and Technology Integration

At the time of publication, the following resources were available (ASCD stock numbers in parentheses).

Classroom Technology Tips (Quick Reference Guide) by Monica Burns (#QRG120045)

The Differentiated Classroom: Responding to the Needs of All Learners, 2nd Edition by Carol Ann Tomlinson (#108029)

Differentiation in Middle and High School: Strategies to Engage All Learners by Kristina J. Doubet & Jessica A. Hockett (#115008)

Differentiation in the Elementary Grades: Strategies to Engage and Equip All Learners by Kristina J. Doubet & Jessica A. Hockett (#117014)

EdTech Essentials: 12 Strategies for Every Classroom in the Age of AI, 2nd Edition by Monica Burns (#124028)

Five Myths About Classroom Technology: How do we integrate digital tools to truly enhance learning? (ASCD Arias) by Matt Renwick (#SF115069E4)

Generating Formative Feedback (Quick Reference Guide) by Jackie Acree Walsh (#QRG122060)

How to Differentiate Instruction in Academically Diverse Classrooms, 3rd Edition by Carol Ann Tomlinson (# 117032)

Improving Student Collaboration with Flexible Grouping (Quick Reference Guide) by Kristina J. Doubet (#QRG122049)

Leading and Managing a Differentiated Classroom, 2nd Edition by Carol Ann Tomlinson and Marcia B. Imbeau (#122012)

So Each May Soar: The Principles and Practices of Learner-Centered Classrooms by Carol Ann Tomlinson (#118006)

Tasks Before Apps: Designing Rigorous Learning in a Tech-Rich Classroom by Monica Burns (#118019)

Teaching for Deeper Learning: Tools to Engage Students in Meaning Making by Jay McTighe

Teaching Up to Reach Each Student (Quick Reference Guide) by Carol Ann Tomlinson (#QRG123035)

Understanding Differentiated Instruction (Quick Reference Guide) by Carol Ann Tomlinson (#QRG117094)

Using AI Chatbots to Enhance Planning and Instruction (Quick Reference Guide) by Monica Burns (#QRG123066)

For up-to-date information about ASCD resources, go to www.ascd.org. You can search the complete archives of *Educational Leadership* at www.ascd.org/el. To contact us, send an email to member@ascd.org or call 1-800-933-2723 or 703-578-9600.